TARAWA

A Battle Report

IRVING WERSTEIN

TARAWA

A Battle Report

MAPS BY AVA MORGAN

THOMAS Y. CROWELL COMPANY: *New York*

By the Author

THE BATTLE OF MIDWAY

THE BATTLE OF AACHEN

GUADALCANAL

WAKE *The Story of a Battle*

TARAWA *A Battle Report*

This book is dedicated
to the memory of
JOHN AUGUSTIN
—talented writer,
gallant soldier,
and fine friend . . .

"This division was especially chosen . . . for the assault on Tarawa. . . . We are the first American troops to attack a defended atoll. . . . I know that you are well trained and fit for the tasks assigned you. . . . Good luck and God bless you all. . . ."

Julian C. Smith
Major General, U.S. Marine Corps
Commanding 2nd Marine Division

NOVEMBER, 1943

"A million men could not take Tarawa in a hundred years!"

Keiji Shibasaki
Rear Admiral, Japanese Imperial Navy
Commanding Tarawa Defense

NOVEMBER, 1943

AUTHOR'S NOTE

During the third week of November, 1943, as Americans all over the United States were readying Thanksgiving turkeys for the traditional holiday feast, newspapers blazoned word of a battle fought and won by the U.S. Marines in the Central Pacific.

The Marines had captured an atoll called Tarawa in the Gilbert Islands. Few Americans had ever heard of the Gilberts, let alone Tarawa or the tiny island named Betio on which the fighting had taken place.

The American people did not realize the importance of the battle that had been won at what seemed disproportionately large Marine casualties. Sensational newspapers spoke of "Tragic Tarawa" and editorials denounced the American attack as another "Charge of the Light Brigade" in which "someone had blundered."

"Our boys died for a few acres of worthless coral," claimed a New York tabloid. "Who thought up this stupid operation? Why were our boys' lives thrown away?"

During the second year of American participation in World War II, such talk seemed perilously close to treason; few of the editorial writers who wrote such inflammatory articles understood the reasons for the attack on Tarawa. The armchair strategists knew nothing about the actual situation.

While it was true that Tarawa exacted a high cost in American casualties, the battle was a cruel, but necessary step in the struggle against Japan.

Tarawa was the first place in the Pacific where the enemy stoutly opposed an amphibious landing; our men had to learn, in battle, the ways to fight a strongly entrenched foe on a fortified coral atoll.

Military and naval leaders had to discover the best means of coping with reefs and tides, of conducting naval bombardments and air strikes on the objective; weapons and amphibious equipment had to be tested in actual combat.

As a result of Tarawa, new tactics, weapons, landing craft, and communications devices were developed. The lives lost at Tarawa saved tenfold their number in later battles along the grimly fought road to Japan.

It is the purpose of this book to re-create the fighting on Betio, the key island of Tarawa Atoll. I have not tried to soft-pedal the struggle, nor have I sought to emphasize its horrors.

My aim is to illuminate the agonies of war for a generation of readers too young to have known the terrors of twenty-odd years ago. It is my hope that today's generation and future ones will be spared the ordeals of the recent past.

Perhaps a recounting of what young men and women faced in the 1940's may make some readers see that the privileges they now enjoy were gained through sacrifice. Perhaps by reading about Tarawa, today's youth may understand that wars are futile. Peaceable methods of settling international difficulties are better than war.

However, peace is not easily kept; free peoples must be prepared to fight for their liberties and freedoms. And in a nation where freedom is cherished, each individual must safeguard the rights of every other one—for where one man is not free, all will eventually become enslaved.

I wish to thank the many people who helped me gather material for this book. Certain persons whose desire to remain anonymous I will respect provided me with letters, journals, diaries, and recollections of the battle for Tarawa. Men, now middle-aged, who had fought on Betio or served aboard ships during the fighting there, reached back into memory and told me graphic stories about the perils and adventures of those hectic days.

I thank them with all my heart. It could not have been easy to dredge up the fury of Tarawa.

I. W.

CONTENTS

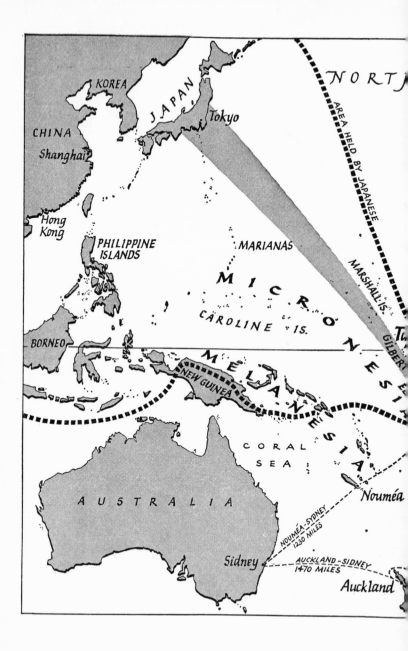

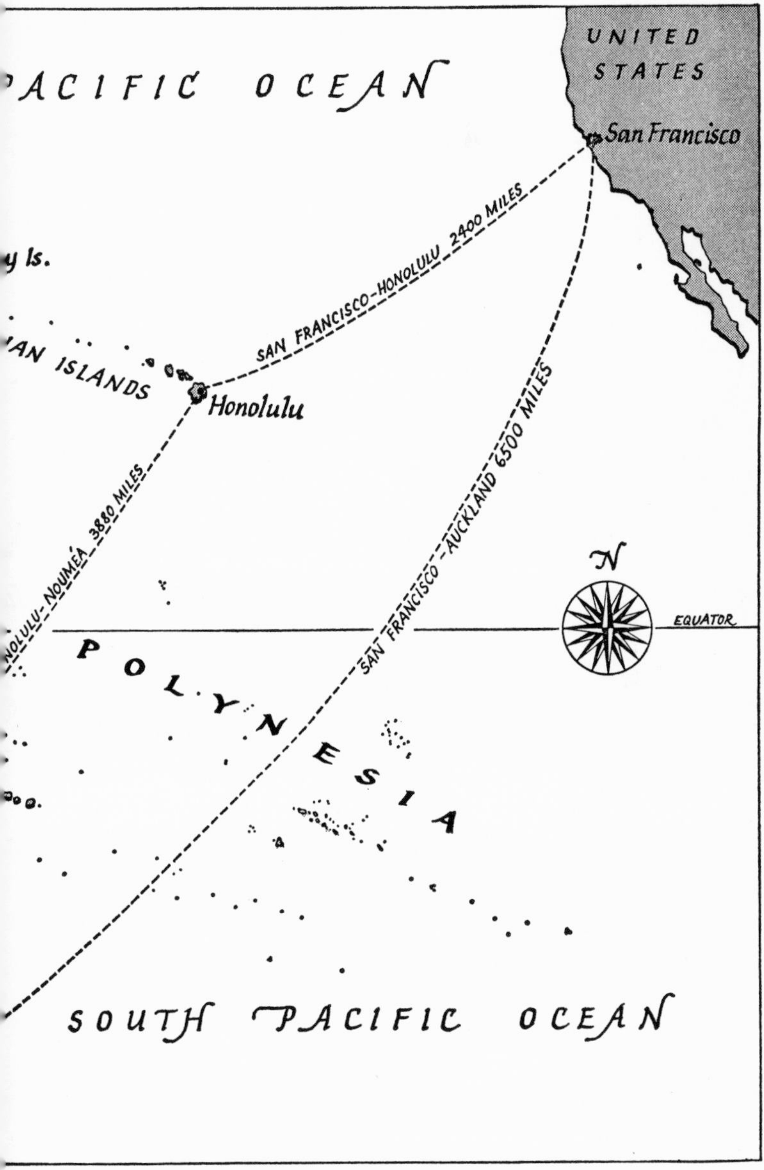

PACIFIC OCEAN
UNITED STATES
San Francisco
SAN FRANCISCO-HONOLULU 2400 MILES
y Is.
IAN ISLANDS
Honolulu
NOLULU-NOUMÉA 3880 MILES
SAN FRANCISCO-AUCKLAND 6500 MILES
N
EQUATOR
POLYNESIA
SOUTH PACIFIC OCEAN

CHAPTER ONE

BETIO

NOVEMBER, 1943

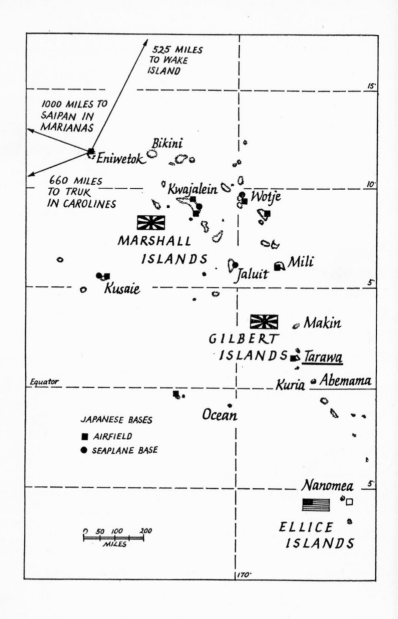

525 MILES TO WAKE ISLAND

1000 MILES IN SAIPAN IN MARIANAS

660 MILES TO TRUK IN CAROLINES

Eniwetok

Bikini

15'

Kwajalein

Wotje

MARSHALL ISLANDS

10'

Jaluit

Mili

Kusaie

5'

Makin

GILBERT ISLANDS

Tarawa

Equator

Kuria

Abemama

Ocean

JAPANESE BASES

■ AIRFIELD

● SEAPLANE BASE

Nanomea

5'

ELLICE ISLANDS

0 50 100 200
MILES

170'

ONE

 1

Rear Admiral Keiji Shibasaki, Imperial Japanese Navy, looked upon himself as a fortunate man. Fate had been kind to him. In a period when he might have been shipped off to New Guinea or some other disease-ridden jungle pesthole such as Guadalcanal, where so many of his fellow officers had met their deaths, the Imperial High Command had sent him to command the defenses in the Gilbert Islands. That Japanese outpost was an archipelago some 2,400 miles southwest of Hawaii in the Central Pacific area.

Shibasaki recited an extra prayer to his ancestors when he drew the assignment. The Gilberts lay in a region where malaria, dengue fever, and jungle rot were unknown. The islands had neither deadly snakes nor poisonous insects; the weather was almost flawless the year round; best of all, the islands had no dank jungle or fetid swamp. Coconut palms and thick, leafy foliage flourished there. In comparison with most Pacific islands, the Gilberts were a tropical paradise —the fabulous South Sea Islands immortalized in fiction and song.

Even while he glowed over his good luck, Shibasaki realized that his selection for the post had not been all based on happy circumstance or mere chance. Very few ranking naval officers were graduate engineers capable of supervising the completion of the Gilbert Islands defensive works. The only colleague whose qualifications equaled his own, Shibasaki recalled, was Rear Admiral Tomanari Saichiro, the very man he had relieved.

Thus, because he had had the foresight to study military, naval, and structural engineering at the University of Tokyo, Shibasaki had received the Gilberts command. At a few minutes before midnight, Friday, November 19, 1943, the admiral stood atop a seawall made of coconut palm logs and admired the moonlight shimmering in the lagoon of Tarawa Atoll, largest of the sixteen island groups that comprised the Gilberts. While it was true that American planes and ships had already struck at Tarawa, the Japanese commander was not unduly concerned. He felt his men could repel any invader.

Out beyond the lagoon lay the coral reef which encircled Tarawa; and, from where he was standing, Shibasaki could see the surf breaking against the saw-toothed coral ledge. At low tide the reef was dry and served to link the twenty-

five coral sand islets that made up L–shaped Tarawa Atoll.
One could actually walk from islet to islet along the jagged
reef.

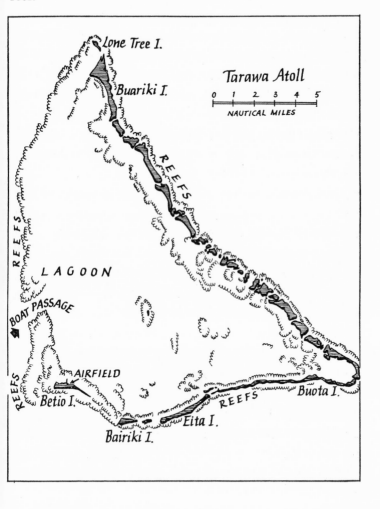

Tarawa Atoll

Admiral Shibasaki was enjoying moonlight and the view from the seawall on Betio—the biggest of Tarawa's components—and the atoll's westernmost point. Some six miles north of Betio the coral reef was broken by a deep, fairly wide channel, which permitted ships of any size to enter the lagoon. Two and one-half miles long and 600 yards deep at the widest point, Betio resembled a bird lying on its back, the beak pointed westward, the tail tapering off to the east.

Because Betio was large enough to hold an airfield, it was made the hub of Tarawa's defenses. Since a seaborne enemy could enter the lagoon only by way of the western channel through the reef, Betio was the key to Tarawa, which in turn served as the Gilberts' main bastion. Should Betio fall, then Tarawa must surrender. If that happened, the Gilbert Islands would be lost. It was Shibasaki's job to see that this never took place.

For many years Betio had been the center of the copra trade in the Gilbert Islands. That industry was the mainstay for the 140 whites and 3,000 Micronesians who inhabited Tarawa Atoll. (Some fishing was done on a commercial basis in the Gilberts but copra was the archipelago's prime stock-in-trade.) Shortly after World War I, an English copra trading firm, Burns Philp Company, set up shop on Betio; the company built an office and a warehouse with a 500-yard-long pier jutting from the loading platform into the lagoon.

At the outbreak of World War II about 26,000 Micronesians lived in almost total obscurity on the Gilbert Islands;
the outside world cared little and knew almost nothing
about the Gilberts. But during the war the once ignored
islands rose to first-class strategic status and received much
attention from both Japanese and Allies.

With the Marshall, Caroline, and Mariana islands, the
Gilberts formed Micronesia, or the "tiny islands." (Other
Pacific island groups were known as Polynesia—"many is-
lands" and Melanesia—"black men's islands.")

Micronesia sprawled astride the sea lanes between the
United States, the Philippines, China, and Japan. By con-
trolling the Gilberts, Marshalls, Carolines, and Marianas,
the Japanese virtually dominated the vast Central Pacific.
Kwajalein in the Marshalls, Truk in the Carolines, and
Saipan in the Marianas were major installations where
planes, ships, and supplies could be concentrated without
fear of Allied aerial reconnaissance.

Those bases were far beyond the range of 1942–1943
type World War II bombers which had to fly from airfields too distant for a raid on Truk, Kwajalein, or other
Japanese strongholds in Micronesia. The only way for the
Americans to get at the enemy was by carrier strikes or else
to gain bases closer in.

It was vital for the U.S. to hit the enemy in Micronesia.
Truk was the site of the biggest Japanese naval base in the
Pacific; airfields on Saipan and Guam defended the ap-

proaches to the Philippines; troops, planes, and ships in the Marshalls threatened the flank of any westward American drive, while the Gilberts were "a dagger aimed at the heart of the U.S.–Australia lifeline," according to Admiral Chester W. Nimitz, the U.S. Commander-in-Chief in the Pacific (CINCPAC).

Japan had wrested the Marianas, Carolines, and Marshalls from Germany during the early months of the First World War. In 1920, she was given control of them under a League of Nations mandate. The mandate terms expressly forbade any military use of the islands but the Imperial High Command flouted this restriction. Japan's militarists lowered a "silken curtain" of secrecy around the islands. For many years no foreign vessel was permitted entry into any of the Mariana, Caroline, or Marshall harbors or lagoons.

Security was so rigidly enforced that alien nationals could not visit the islands even as passengers aboard Japanese ships. Consequently, no Westerner had knowledge of the seaplane bases, airfields, submarine pens, barracks, and naval stations under construction in the formerly peaceful islands where the Rising Sun flag now flew.

In December, 1941, when Japan launched the Pacific War, the Imperial Navy attacked Pearl Harbor and Wake Island from bases in the Marshalls. The submarines that penetrated Pearl Harbor on December 7, 1941, had sortied out of Kwajalein as had the men who captured Wake.

Bombers from Roi and Wotje in the Marshalls blasted Wake Island. Warships of the Imperial Navy's Fourth Fleet refueled and armed at Truk and Kwajalein. Japan was taking full advantage of the islands which the League of Nations had so naively turned over to her.

The Japanese-held Micronesian islands were strongly fortified with coast artillery, antiaircraft batteries, and a variety of machine guns. Pillboxes and bunkers made miniature fortresses of the tiny coral sand isles. The Mikado's war planners had done their jobs well.

While the Western powers dozed and dallied, the Japanese spent almost twenty years readying the Carolines, Marianas, and Marshalls for a Pacific conflict. Japan's war power was a monstrous octopus straddling the Central Pacific, with tentacles reaching out in almost every direction.

However, the Japanese warhawks were not quite satisfied with their position; a portion of Micronesia had escaped their grasp. The Gilbert, Ellice, Phoenix, Union, and Ocean islands had belonged to the British for decades. With a governmental seat located on Ocean Island, the Gilbert and Ellice Islands Crown Colony (which included Phoenix and Union islands) was proclaimed in 1892.

The Gilberts were named for Captain Thomas Gilbert, master of the merchantman *Charlotte,* who had discovered the archipelago in 1788. During his cruise Captain Gilbert charted a number of the islands that made up the group. Among these islands were the following: Abemama,

Kuria, Aranuka, Tarawa, Abaiang, Butaritari, and Makin.

About fifty years later, Lieutenant Charles Wilkes, U.S. Navy, commanding the *Peacock* on a voyage of exploration and discovery in the Central Pacific, came on the Gilberts. He landed at Tarawa and drew up a chart of the atoll with such accuracy that it was still used by seamen a century afterward. Wilkes also recorded for posterity that Gilbertese women were "the comeliest females in the South Seas. . . . The men were quite handsome and well-muscled. . . . They had a fierce and warlike nature at times and armed themselves with ten-foot-long spears that had sharks' teeth heads. . . ."

For a time after Wilkes' journey, scant notice was paid the Gilbert Islands. Occasionally a trading schooner put in at Tarawa, usually landing at Betio. Schooners stopped off at the other atolls as well and generally the natives received their visitors in a friendly manner, but once in a while a seaman would be killed for violating a tribal tabu or molesting a Micronesian woman.

In the mid-nineteenth century Protestant missionaries flocked to the Gilberts and converted the natives to Christianity. Close behind the Protestants came Roman Catholic priests. Before long the clergymen had persuaded most islanders to surrender their pagan ways. (A survey made just before World War II revealed that about 43 percent of the Gilbertese were Protestant; 34 percent practiced Catholicism and the remaining 23 percent still worshiped ancient gods, practiced pagan rites, and performed ages-old rituals.)

Under British rule the Gilbertese prospered and multiplied. By 1941, the islanders numbered more than 26,000 contented men, women, and children. (Included in that number were a dozen American Negroes who seemed to have found happiness in the islands.) The Gilberts were the most densely populated area in the Central Pacific. The British colonial administration wisely gave the islanders a good deal of self-rule. Each village had its own *kaubure,* or council, which governed as it had through numberless centuries.

The people led a fairly tranquil existence. Life was good in the Gilberts. No one worked hard. No one had great wealth. No one was in want. Crime was almost unknown. From cradle to grave the Gilbert Islanders lived happily as British subjects.

But this serene period ended abruptly. On December 10, 1941, only three days after they had started World War II in the Pacific, the Japanese swooped down out of the Marshalls to seize Makin, Tarawa, and other Gilbert Island atolls.

This aggression at the outbreak of the Pacific war started a chain of events which eventually brought Rear Admiral Shibasaki to tiny Betio Island where he was fated to lead his countrymen in one of the bloodiest battles fought during the Pacific War. . . .

≣ ||||||| 2

For several months after they had taken the Gilberts, the Japanese left only token forces scattered throughout the islands. The largest unit garrisoned Tarawa and had its headquarters on Betio.

Except for a change in rulers, most Gilbertese went on as they had in the past. Indeed, there were not enough Japanese in the islands to make much difference. The only obvious change was the Rising Sun flag fluttering from the administration building on Betio where once the Union Jack had flown.

After a while, life was drastically altered for the natives of Betio, where the greatest number of Japanese troops were stationed. The soldiers treated the Gilbertese harshly. They annoyed girls and women, beat up the men, and forced everyone to work at digging trenches, foxholes, and gun emplacements.

At first, the only major military installation that the Imperial High Command constructed in the Gilberts was a seaplane base on Butaritari Island of Makin Atoll. Seaplanes taking off from there could harass shipping lanes to Australia.

The Americans were gravely concerned about the Japanese hold on the Gilberts. Something dramatic had to be done about this threat to the U.S.–Australia lifeline. Action was taken in August, 1942.

While fighting raged on Guadalcanal, units of the 2nd Marine Raider Battalion led by Lieutenant Colonel Evans P. Carlson boarded the long-range submarines *Nautilus* and *Argonaut* at Pearl Harbor and headed for Makin Atoll. On the night of August 17 the submarines surfaced off Butaritari Island, and Carlson's Raiders sneaked ashore in rubber boats.

They caught the Japanese by surprise. The hard-hitting Leathernecks blew up a radio transmitter; wrecked seaplane moorings and ramps with explosives; and destroyed fuel tanks, repair sheds, and other installations. At small loss to themselves they killed or wounded more than 100 Japanese. Upon finishing their work of devastation, the Raiders piled back into their rubber boats and paddled out to the submarines which carried them safely away.

Carlson's daring feat won big headlines back in the United States. In that grim August of 1942, the country yearned for good news. The war was an oppressive burden on Americans not accustomed to rationing of food, clothing, and gasoline. Even worse, Americans were unprepared psychologically for the suffering and sacrifice of war. They had forgotten the lesson of their past that nothing can be won without struggle; there is no quick and sure formula for victory.

But the raid on Butaritari seemed to disprove all that. Why, they had the Japs on the ropes! They'd hit 'em where it hurt! So the headlines were huge, and radio commenta-

13

tors raved on about the significance of Carlson's deed. One sagely predicted that the Japanese could not "withstand another such setback. . . ."

"A couple of more wallops like this and Tojo'll be down for the count," a widely read columnist wrote in a leading New York tabloid. The victory-starved American public inflated the minor incident on that distant coral island to the proportions and importance of a second Gettysburg. In fact, one noted journalist called Carlson's raid "the turning point in the Pacific."

There was no basis for the optimism that swept the United States after Makin. Carlson's action was a mere flicker in the darkness and not a glaring beam. Civilian joy soon diminished as the truth became apparent. The raid had been a pinprick, not a mortal stab.

In military circles there was some cynicism about the wisdom of the hit-and-run attack. Marine Corps Major General Holland M. Smith labeled the effort a "piece of downright foolishness." He contended that the raid had accomplished nothing except to "shoot up a few Nips and throw such a scare into Tojo that he'll try to turn the Gilberts into a Gibraltar. . . ."

General Smith's conclusion was a sound one. The startled enemy had believed the Gilberts to be out of American reach; now, the Imperial High Command had been warned. The islands were vulnerable and Tokyo intended to do something to remedy the situation.

The High Command decided to make Betio the heart of the Gilberts' defense. By mid-September, troops and equipment poured onto that island. Pioneer troops began building fortifications under the direction of Rear Admiral Tomanari Saichiro. Thus the net results of Carlson's raid were to build up Japanese power in the Gilberts and make Betio an almost impregnable stronghold.

A tireless, wiry little man, Admiral Saichiro exuded energy. He kept the 1,247 men of the 111th Pioneers at work on a round-the-clock schedule. The hard-working Japanese built an airfield on the western half of Betio at the bird-shaped islet's widest part. Saichiro mapped out a defense

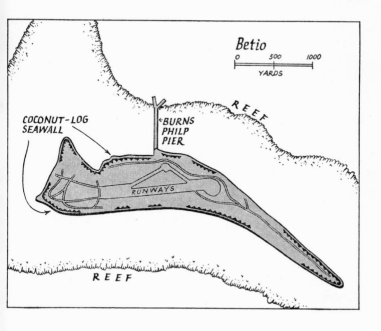

network aimed at annihilating an enemy's thrust. Since no part of Betio was more than 300 yards from the beach, almost every weapon on the island could be brought to bear on an invader attempting to land.

Each of Betio's 291 acres bristled with every size and caliber gun in the Japanese arsenal. They poked out of firing slits in sturdy steel-and-concrete pillboxes, bunkers, and blockhouses. The island was studded with vast two-story-high bombproof shelters, one of which served as the island's command post.

Saichiro erected a coconut-log seawall that girdled the landing beaches. The wall stood about 20 yards inland and ranged from three to five feet in height. The only way off the beach was to climb the wall. An invader scrambling over it made an easy target for riflemen and machine gunners hidden amid coconut palms and shrubbery on the far side of the wall.

Should an enemy take cover behind the log barricade, he would be raked by shells from well-placed mortars zeroed in on the beach. Light artillery, as well as mortars, was positioned to sweep the sands on the wall's beach side.

Saichiro personally supervised the placement of every gun on Betio. He wore himself out inspecting all the positions—and there were many. No less than 62 heavy and 44 light machine guns covered the beaches. Nine 37-mm anti-tank guns and 37-mm cannon stripped from 14 light tanks had been dug into the coral and expertly camouflaged.

16

Added to this array of automatic weapons and light artillery were the rifles, grenades, bayonets, pistols, and submachine guns of the island's garrison, the Sasebo 7th Special Naval Landing Force (Imperial Marines) and the 3rd Special Base Force (another crack unit of Imperial Marines). These were tough, cocky, and hardened troops, the cream of Japan's fighting men.

Tank traps were dug at each end of the airfield. The landing strip was protected by rifle pits and coconut-log pillboxes from which an interlaced fire could be unleashed. All positions were linked by communication trenches.

Admiral Saichiro also had heavy artillery on his island fortress. There were six 70-mm guns; eight 75-mm antiaircraft (AA) guns; ten 75-mm mountain howitzers; four 5-inch coastal guns; six 80-mm AA guns; four 5.5-inch and four 8-inch coastal guns that had been hauled from Singapore to Betio.

The 70-mm, 75-mm, and 80-mm AA guns could also be used as anti-boat (AB) weapons. They were splendidly positioned and given predesignated fields of fire. The guns and their crews were protected by concrete and coral-block emplacements.

The 5-, 5.5- and 8-inchers could slug it out with an invasion fleet at a range of up to 15,000 yards. The 8-inchers —two at each end of the island—were served from huge concrete ammunition bunkers.

Admiral Saichiro remained on Betio for eleven months,

17

until August, 1943. Although his strength and energy were spent, the admiral was well pleased; he had almost completed his mission of turning tiny Betio into an impressive bastion. But Saichiro had gone beyond his physical limits and was unable to continue the task. The job was passed on to Rear Admiral Keiji Shibasaki who came to Betio in mid-August.

The new CO saw that the only work his predecessor had left undone was the placing of mines and other obstructions in the waters surrounding Betio. Saichiro had been kept so busy with the guns, pillboxes, and blockhouses that his time had run out before he could start the water defense.

Shibasaki began at once to remedy that deficiency. Off the southern shore of Betio (the ocean side) he planted an obstacle maze of pyramidal-shaped concrete slabs, known as "tetrahedrons," wired together, with mines scattered between the rows. The tetrahedrons were placed in a pattern that would force incoming boats into a pointblank barrage from the 70-mm, 75-mm, and 80-mm cannon plus the concentrated fire of numerous machine guns.

By the middle of September, work was completed off Betio's southern beaches. Shibasaki had only to secure, in a similar fashion, the northern (lagoon) beaches and the landing area (ocean) to the west. He intended to obstruct and mine the lagoon from the beach out to the coral reef 500 to 1,000 yards away.

Shibasaki could relax once the lagoon was properly safeguarded. Then, if the Yankees were stupid enough to attack Betio, they would meet total annihilation—*zemmetsu*. The admiral sensed that an attack was probable in that autumn of 1943. The Yankees were daily growing more and more aggressive.

From its outset, the year had portended evil for Nippon. The ancient war gods seemed to be frowning on the Sons of Heaven. In February, 1943, the Americans had finally won the struggle on Guadalcanal. Then, in April, another cruel blow had fallen on Japan: Yankee assassins in P-38 (Lightning) planes over Bougainville had ambushed a "Betty" bomber carrying Fleet Admiral Isoroku Yamamoto, Commander-in-Chief, Imperial Japanese Navy. Yamamoto, hailed as Japan's "best military thinker," was killed. He had masterminded the attack on Pearl Harbor; all the Imperial Navy's brilliant victories had been his brainchildren. His loss was grievous for Japan.

Even more disconcerting than Yamamoto's death was the Japanese fear that, somehow, Yankee agents had penetrated the highest war councils. The Fleet Admiral's trip to Bougainville had been a secret known only to a few staff officers. Yet, the P-38's had been lurking at the precise place and time to waylay Yamamoto. Japanese counterintelligence operatives frantically hunted for nonexistent American spies, only to meet utter frustration.

(The Japanese did not then know, nor did they learn until after the war was over, that U.S. Naval Intelligence

19

had broken the Imperial Navy's radio code and, thus, had learned about Yamamoto's trip.)

Japan had been forced on the defensive in this second autumn of the Pacific conflict. She was losing ground on all fronts. The Americans had recaptured Attu and Kiska in the North Pacific Aleutian Islands. The New Guinea campaign was going badly for Japan in the face of a U.S.–Australian offensive led by General Douglas MacArthur. That doughty officer was also preparing moves elsewhere; an American attack had already started in the Solomons with a mighty blow against Bougainville.

This was the time of trial for Japan, and the Imperial High Command braced itself to take the shock. Before coming to Betio, Admiral Shibasaki had been briefed on top leadership strategy—a plan called Yogaki.

Yogaki worked on the assumption that the Americans intended launching a series of "island hopping" offensives to capture one Japanese base after another in the South and Central Pacific theaters. Once this was accomplished, the Yankees would make a massive effort to retake the Philippines, and then aim an all-out assault on Japan itself.

Under Yogaki, every Japanese-held atoll would be strongly defended, particularly in the Marshalls and Gilberts, the outermost Japanese bastions. Every islet they captured must be made to cost the Americans so much in men, ships, and planes that they could not afford to press the attacks.

20

Yogaki is the Japanese word for attrition.

"We shall bleed the Yankees dry," boasted an officer of the Imperial High Command.

Having been alerted by Carlson's raid on Makin Atoll, the Japanese war planners surmised that the Gilberts would be one of the first American targets in the Central Pacific. Since Tarawa Atoll was more defensible than Makin or other islands in the Gilberts, Admiral Saichiro, and then Admiral Shibasaki, continued to fortify Betio.

The High Command assured Shibasaki that should the Americans attack, he would be backed by planes, ships, submarines, and troops. Long-range aircraft from Rabaul would blast the invader's ships. Zero fighter planes would guard against U.S. carrier-based aircraft. The Imperial Navy's Second Fleet under Admiral Nobutake Kondo was primed to speed down from Truk to engage any U.S. naval force in a surface battle. At the same time, swarms of submarines were to converge on Betio from all directions and torpedo every American ship in sight.

If the enemy did not yet know of Yogaki, he could most easily learn about it by attacking Betio. "We have prepared a hornets' nest for the Yankees," declared an aide to Fleet Admiral Miniechi Koga, Yamamoto's successor.

However, the hornets did not sting the Americans, and the elaborately detailed Yogaki plan began to fall to pieces.

On September 18–19, the fast new U.S. carriers *Lexington, Princeton,* and *Belleau Wood,* having sneaked up on Betio, unleashed a series of savage air strikes. Dauntless (SBD) and Helldiver (SB2C) bombers, escorted by Hellcat (F6F) fighters, swarmed over the island at daybreak. Within minutes, 9 of Betio's 18 planes were in flames on the ground and the rest damaged beyond repair. Barges loaded with cement for the tetrahedrons were sunk. The hail of bombs and bullets also killed and wounded a number of Imperial Marines.

From the American point of view, however, the raid's most important result was not the damage but a set of excellent photos snapped by reconnaissance fliers off the flattop *Lexington.* The pictures of Betio's northern (lagoon) side proved invaluable in mapping the invasion.

The furious aerial assault shook Admiral Shibasaki, but he soon saw that nothing fatal had occurred. The loss of the cement barges was serious. Now there would be no obstacles in the lagoon. But that did not worry Shibasaki too much. With the approach of autumn, a seasonal low neap tide peculiar to the Gilbert Islands was at hand, a condition that lasted until late November when spring tide flooded the beaches up to the seawall.

During the neap, the water seldom rose higher than one to three feet over the inner lagoon reef, and often even less. This meant the Americans could not cross the coral barrier in landing craft. Nature would keep the Yankees out of the

22

lagoon even more effectively than all the tetrahedrons and mines. Besides, the air raids, though severe, had left unscathed most gun emplacements, bunkers, and pillboxes.

"Let the Yankees come," Shibasaki told an aide. "A million men could not take Tarawa in a hundred years!"

His boastfulness leaned heavily on the help he expected under Yogaki. But the Americans, who had never even heard of the plan, shattered it beyond repair when U.S. Marines stormed Bougainville on November 1, and the troops Shibasaki had been counting on were rushed to hold the Solomons instead.

Four days later, bombers from the flattops *Saratoga* and *Princeton* struck Rabaul and obliterated the cruisers of the Imperial Second Fleet. These ships had been the backbone of Admiral Kondo's force. Now he could no longer come to Shibasaki's aid.

More bad news harried that unhappy officer. A second U.S. carrier force bombed Rabaul again on November 11 and, before that raid ended, 90 Japanese fighter planes had been shot down or destroyed on the ground. These lost aircraft had been earmarked for the defense of Betio. With this dark tiding came word that the Imperial submarine fleet had suffered grave setbacks. Instead of wolf-packs to patrol the area around the Gilberts, Shibasaki could expect only a few submarines, if any.

In short, Yogaki had been scrapped. It was left to the more than 4,000 Imperial Marines on Betio to throw the

23

Yankees into the sea without any support from outside. Shibasaki was convinced that the Americans were going to come in force very soon. The tempo of Yankee air attacks on Betio speeded up. Since Saturday, November 13, daily aerial strikes had been made on Betio by carrier-based planes and Liberator bombers from the U.S. Army Air Corps base on Funafuti Atoll in the Ellice Islands, 704 miles to the south.

The island's defenders stood a 24-hour alert. Betio's AA guns blazed away by the hour, but without success; no American planes were brought down, although several suffered shrapnel damage. At night, sentries kept a sharp lookout for an invasion fleet.

By sunset Friday, November 19, instinct told Admiral Shibasaki that the invasion was at hand. "I feel it in my bones," he told a fellow officer. "In a day, maybe less, we will be fighting for our lives."

Since he had no scout planes to seek out approaching American ships, Shibasaki could only guess at their proximity. The presence of American warships became a known fact in the late afternoon of the 19th when three U.S. cruisers and two destroyers suddenly appeared to pound Betio with salvo after salvo.

When the ships drew off at sunset, Shibasaki issued a message to his troops:

> *I order you, in the Emperor's name, to defend to*
> *the last man all vital areas. Should the enemy*

attempt a landing, destroy him at the water's edge. I know you will not fail our Emperor, Hirohito, the Son of Heaven! Banzai! Long live Japan!

After delivering this ringing order, Shibasaki retired to his command post and mulled over his situation. The series of air raids plus the naval bombardment had put out of commission the 8-inch battery on the western tip of the island. Those guns were to have covered the passageway through the outer coral reef barrier. Several smaller artillery pieces also had been knocked out. Casualties among the troops remained low; the men had kept under cover and only a few had been killed or wounded.

The worst aspect of the raids had been the depletion of ammunition stores. Thousands of rounds were used shooting at Yankee aircraft. Now, an acute shortage of antiaircraft and machine-gun ammunition faced Shibasaki, but his confidence remained unshaken.

That midnight, as the admiral stood on the seawall looking out across the silvery lagoon, he did not know that zero hour had almost come. An American armada of 3 battleships, 5 cruisers, 9 destroyers, and 16 cargo ships, carrying more than 16,000 men of the 2nd U.S. Marine Division, was closing in on Betio.

The men and ships were part of Operation Galvanic, the most ambitious U.S. effort in the Pacific War up to that point. Operation Galvanic was the code name for a two-

25

pronged attack in the Gilberts: the northern wing aimed at Makin Atoll; the southern, more powerful, wing to crush the Japanese on Betio and drive the enemy from Tarawa and the Gilberts.

Before the sun rose Saturday, November 20, Admiral Shibasaki and every man on Betio would face the full impact of Operation Galvanic. But as the midnight breeze whispered in the palm trees and the yellow moon shone down, Admiral Shibasaki had no tangible evidence that something so momentous was astir and yet he felt uneasy, and confided to an aide waiting nearby, "Our moment of destiny is at hand. We are pawns in a monstrous chess game. It is good to die for the Emperor. There is no more becoming way to give up one's life. Remember, when the fatal second comes, that honor is sweeter than life. We shall meet our destiny like warriors of Japan with the courage and faith of Samurai."

He then turned from the seawall and trudged toward his command post bunker, noting, as he passed, the sentries patrolling their posts and the gun crews standing by.

Betio was ready, no matter what lay ahead. . . .

CHAPTER TWO

OPERATION GALVANIC

NOVEMBER, 1943

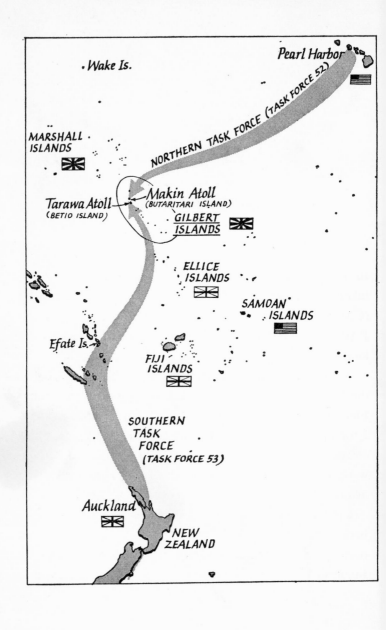

TWO

≣ ‖‖‖‖‖   1

In February, 1943, shortly after Guadalcanal had been taken, Admiral Ernest King, Chief of Naval Operations (CNO), suggested to Admiral Chester W. Nimitz (CINC-PAC) that an assault be mounted against the Gilbert Islands.

Nimitz liked the idea, but felt it was premature because the Central Pacific Force (Fifth Fleet) of the U.S. Pacific Fleet, consisting of old battleships, several aircraft carriers, a few cruisers, and some battered destroyers, was not strong enough to carry out a major amphibious operation. Nor were sufficient ground troops, trained in landing tactics, yet available.

CINCPAC did not scuttle the offensive against the Gilberts, but merely tabled it for a while. Nimitz had good reasons for wanting to take the Gilbert Islands. Back in January, U.S. Army Liberator (B-24) bombers equipped with special cameras had carried out a combination photo-bombing mission over Tarawa. The developed films caused concern at CINCPAC headquarters in Pearl Harbor. The pictures revealed that the Japanese had not only con-structed an airfield on Betio, but also were fortifying the islet. Another Liberator group flew a similar mission over Makin Atoll. Their photos showed that the enemy had built a first-class seaplane base on Butaritari Island to replace the crude installations Carlson's Raiders had demolished in August, 1942.

Nimitz realized that he could not allow the Japanese a free hand in the Gilberts much longer. If the enemy con-tinued to work unhampered, "he will make the Gilberts impregnable . . . something must be done soon," CINC-PAC wrote CNO.

Naval Intelligence provided still another reason for in-vading the Gilberts. One of the islands, Abemama, a lan-guid tropical hideaway some 75 miles southeast of Tarawa, was a suitable site for an airstrip. A field on Abemama, plus the one on Betio, spelled big trouble for the Americans.

Admiral Nimitz requested that the Joint Chiefs of Staff (JCS) and Admiral King (CNO) beef up the Fifth Fleet so that it could support an amphibious attack against the Gil-berts. CINCPAC also asked for troops well enough trained to do the job.

The JCS agreed with Nimitz. During June, 1943, the Fifth Fleet began getting modern ships of all types. The

30

brand new flattop *Essex* and the new carriers *Yorktown, Lexington, Independence, Belleau Wood,* and *Princeton,* equipped with the latest type of planes, and accompanied by 20 destroyers plus several cruisers, were assigned to the Central Pacific sector.

The speedy battleships *Alabama* and *South Dakota,* the latter completely refurbished from the damage she had received at Guadalcanal, came to Nimitz in August. By October, the JCS promised, the admiral could expect 5 more recently commissioned battleships and 7 old ones. He would also receive 10 fast carriers, 7 escort carriers, 8 heavy and 4 light cruisers, 66 destroyers, 27 attack transports (APA), and 9 large merchantmen.

All the air power of the Pacific Fleet not assigned to Admiral "Bull" Halsey, then operating in the South Pacific, would be turned over to the Fifth Fleet. The Army's VII Air Force in Hawaii would also cooperate in the Gilberts campaign, which was dubbed with the code name Operation Galvanic. The immediate objectives were to capture Tarawa and Makin atolls.

Now that the Fifth Fleet packed a real punch, Nimitz went ahead full speed with Operation Galvanic. Vice Admiral Raymond A. Spruance, who had beaten the Japanese at Midway, was made Fifth Fleet Commander (CO) on August 15, 1943. Ten days later, the V Amphibious Force was set up as part of the Fifth Fleet. This force, which was immediately nicknamed "V 'Phib," had as its commander

Rear Admiral Richmond Kelly Turner, a veteran of many Pacific battles. The V 'Phib Force consisted of all attack transports (APA), attack cargo vessels (AKA), and landing craft in the Central Pacific.

Turner's flagship was the old battleship *Pennsylvania,* which had been damaged at Pearl Harbor on December 7, 1941. Since that date, the Japanese had reported sinking the *"Pennsy"* so many times that the gallant ship was called "The Gray Ghost of the Pacific."

The V 'Phib was divided into two amphibious groups known as the Northern Attack Force (Task Force 52), commanded by Admiral Turner, and the Southern Attack Force (Task Force 53), under Rear Admiral Harry W. Hill. Task Force (TF) 52 was assigned to capture Makin Atoll while TF 53 was given the invasion of Tarawa as its mission. Admiral Hill's flag flew on the battleship *Maryland.*

All ground troops of V 'Phib were commanded by Major General Holland M. Smith, United States Marine Corps (USMC), a pioneer in the development of equipment and tactics for amphibious operations. It was he who had trained the units that recaptured Attu and Kiska.

A person of uncertain temper, the general was known as "Howlin' Mad" Smith in the Marine Corps. An apparently mild-mannered man, he resembled a small-town real estate broker, with his toothbrush mustache and silver-framed eye glasses.

32

"The old boy wanted things done his way—usually because he was right. He was gentle and soft-spoken until somebody goofed! Then the sparks flew! He'd chew out a man proper, and he was always harder on officers than enlisted men," an aide recalled.

In the weeks that followed, "Howlin' Mad" Smith "blew his top" many times while whipping Operation Galvanic into shape. He was advised by the JCS on September 15 that Tarawa was to be attacked by the 2nd Marine Division, then in Wellington, New Zealand. The outfit had last fought on Guadalcanal. It was commanded by Major General Julian Smith (no relation to "Howlin' Mad").

The 165th Infantry Regiment of the 27th Infantry Division was picked for the Makin invasion. That outfit had gained fame in the past as the "Fighting 69th." A New York National Guard unit, it was made up largely of Irishmen from New York City. Coincidentally, the 27th Division was commanded by Major General Ralph C. Smith, not related to the other two Smiths. The 165th was stationed in Hawaii.

Major General Julian Smith, known as "Uncle" Julian, was a quiet, affable Leatherneck with thirty-four years of service in the Corps. A Marine officer once described him as looking like "the guy next door who spent Saturday night baby-sitting with his grandchildren."

A conscientious man, Julian Smith studied every detail of the mission at his Wellington headquarters. He pored over all available charts and maps he could find of Tarawa. The uncertain tides there worried him. Although the 2nd Marine Division would enter the lagoon by way of the channel through the outer reef, Betio itself was surrounded by an inner (fringing) reef.

The invasion was scheduled for November 20, the period of neap tide, and General Smith was concerned about his men crossing the fringing reef in their landing craft (Higgins Boats). He knew Tarawa was sometimes visited by a high "dodging" tide during the neap period. But its duration was unpredictable; and, since no dependable tide charts existed for Tarawa Atoll, particularly Betio, General Smith consulted with ship captains who had sailed the atoll's waters.

What he learned from them was disconcerting. The skippers told him that odds were against a high "dodger" at Betio on November 20. This could mean the fringing reef might have only a foot or less of water covering the coral on D-Day, not enough to float Higgins Boats.

The troubled general then called for a conference with General Holland M. Smith at Pearl Harbor. There, the 2nd Marine Division's CO voiced his doubts about crossing the fringing reef. Admiral "Kelly" Turner, who was present, tried to reassure him that there would be a high "dodger" on D-Day.

But there was also the possibility that the tide would be low. In that event, "Uncle" Julian pointed out, his men would be forced to crawl across the reef and wade to shore

34

—a distance of more than 500 yards—under fire all the way. He wanted amphibious tractors (amtracs) which could climb the reef and then churn on to the beach. Amtracs—popularly called "alligators"—were officially designated as Landing Vehicles, Tracked (LVT). They were Caterpillar-tread amphibious vehicles, propelled by gasoline engines.

Their advantages over Higgins Boats were numerous, especially for invading a reef-encircled atoll. An alligator had a speed of four knots in the water. It could climb reefs, shoals, and sand bars. On land, an amtrac could tear through barbed wire, scale barricades, straddle ditches, and roll along on level ground at 15 mph.

These ungainly mechanical monsters weighed 23,000 pounds each, and were 25 feet long and 10 feet 8 inches wide. They could carry 25 passengers plus a crew of six; mounting twin .50-caliber machine guns, amtracs could throw a lot of lead as they waddled from water to land.

The 2nd Marine Division had about 75 amtracs of its own, but required another 100 for the invasion according to its CO. At this point in the meeting, General Holland M. Smith confronted Admiral Turner. "How soon can we have the vehicles, Kelly?" he asked.

Turner shook his head. "You don't need them, Holland. There's going to be a high 'dodger' on November 20. Besides, I don't have time to collect amtracs. . . ."

It was then, according to a naval officer attending the conference, that it became clear why Holland M. Smith was called "Howlin' Mad."

"He reared right up, shook his finger under Turner's nose and yelled, 'By thunder, Kelly, I want amtracs and I'll have 'em!' And he kept on shouting like that, pounding the table with his fist, until he was red in the face."

Admiral Turner tried to mollify the choleric Leatherneck. "There's no need to blow up, General. You won't need amtracs. . . ."

"Admiral, don't tell me what I need! You handle your ships, and I'll take care of my men," "Howlin' Mad" shouted. "Julian asked for amtracs and he'll get 'em! I'm telling you straight out, Admiral—either you produce a hundred amtracs or the deal's off! No alligators—no operation. You know me, Kelly. I mean it!"

Turner threw up his hands and sighed wearily. "Yes, General, I know you. I'll rustle up a hundred amtracs for you and find room for them on the ships. Now let's get back to business—there's been enough blab."

"Sure, Kelly, let's get back to business," "Howlin' Mad" said, winking slyly at Julian Smith.

The conference covered many points. The officers discussed Makin, where the 165th Infantry would be confronted by 500 enemy troops according to Intelligence estimates. (Actually twice that many Japanese were on Butaritari.) Operation Galvanic's third Smith (General Ralph C.) was told that his 165th Infantry Regiment, reinforced by artillery, engineers, and demolition specialists, was to be redesignated the 165th Regimental Combat Team (RCT) for this mission.

Plans were also laid for Operation "Boxcloth," which was the seizure of Abemama. On the night of November 20, a 2nd Division Reconnaissance platoon was to sail on the submarine *Nautilus* from Tarawa. The men would land on Abemama by rubber boat. This advance group would then scout out the Japanese defenses and await reinforcements. (Intelligence reported a full Japanese company on Abemama. This was highly inaccurate. Only 23 Japanese Marines defended Abemama.)

For a change, Intelligence proved itself uncannily observant in judging the numbers defending Betio. It was claimed that about 4,500 Imperial Marines and Pioneer troops held that bastion. (A count after the battle showed that the garrison numbered 4,836, including labor troops.)

The planners of Operation Galvanic decided to use only two of the 2nd Division's three regiments in the assault on Betio. The 2nd and 8th Marine Regiments would spearhead the attack while the 6th Marines remained as a mobile reserve under the control of General Holland M. Smith with headquarters on the *Pennsylvania*. Should the 6th Marines be needed, Julian Smith would have to obtain their release from V 'Phib.

However, all the men of the 2nd Marine Division were brought together in the last week of October. The outfit boarded 16 transports at Wellington, New Zealand. The Leathernecks were in high spirits as they trudged up the gangplanks. "Uncle" Julian had announced that the division was to hold maneuvers at Hawkes Bay, about 150 miles north of Wellington. The exercises, he stated, were scheduled to last two weeks. The men were told they would be back in Wellington by mid-November.

Cheering townspeople crowded the docks to wave *au revoir* to the grinning Marines; pretty girls threw kisses to their American boy friends, who reciprocated.

It was a gala and happy time as bands played popular airs on the pier and everybody joined in singing the "Marine Hymn." The transports backed out into the harbor to that stirring refrain.

It was Monday, November 1.

The troop-packed transports made for the open sea where a destroyer division fell in as escort. Only then were the Marines told they were going to Efate in the New Hebrides group to prepare for the attack on Betio Island of Tarawa Atoll in the Gilberts. Only a few high-ranking officers had known all along that the 2nd Marine Division was leaving New Zealand forever.

"A great groan shook our ship when the boys got the word. We cursed and hollered. What a way to leave New Zealand and those wonderful girls!" a Marine recalled many years later.

"I wouldn't have been so sore about leaving if we were

going to fight a battle that meant something. The Solomons, New Guinea, *anywhere!* But none of us had ever heard of Tarawa, much less Betio—and the Gilbert Islands could've been on the moon for all we cared," a Marine complained.

Many men were irked because the truth had been kept from them. "What gives? Doesn't 'Uncle' Julian trust us? We wouldn't have blabbed," a noncom said.

Julian Smith had not acted deviously because he mistrusted his troops. But he remembered what had happened when the 1st Marine Division left Wellington some fifteen months earlier. The local newspapers had run headlines about the forthcoming American attack on Tulagi and Guadalcanal. "Uncle" Julian wanted no repetition of such journalistic irresponsibility. It was hard enough to fight a campaign, without letting the enemy know all about it before time.

For that reason he had cooked up the Hawkes Bay maneuver yarn. The ruse worked so well that the governor general of New Zealand was unaware the 2nd Marine Division was leaving for good until after it had sailed.

When word got out that the Marines were not coming back, an emotional crisis swept Wellington. According to a newspaper report:

> . . . *all the lovely young girls in our fair city seem to be weeping at the news about the Americans. . . . Like Caesar, the Yanks came, saw,*

39

*and conquered . . . now they have left behind
memories, broken hearts, and uncounted extravagant promises . . . perhaps they played fast
and loose with our gullible girls . . . but we wish
them Godspeed and good luck wherever the for-
tunes of war may take them. . . .*

≡ ||||||| 2

About a week before the 2nd Marine division departed
Wellington, Rear Admiral Harry W. Hill ordered Task
Force 53 to sortie out of Pearl Harbor and make for Efate.
Hill's powerful armada—3 battleships, 5 cruisers, 5 escort
carriers, and 21 destroyers—arrived at its destination with-
out incident on November 5.

To Efate also came a cargo ship bringing 50 amtracs
which had been rushed from San Diego, California. More
amtracs were stashed aboard transports and cargo ships.
Although Admiral Turner still insisted there would be a
high "dodger" tide at Betio on D-Day (November 20), he
kept his word to "Howlin' Mad" Smith and produced the
requested amtracs.

In the week that followed, all hands on Efate worked
hard and long. The two assault regiments (2nd and 8th
Marines) engaged in landing practice at Mele Bay. By platoons they clambered down landing nets slung over the
sides of the transports, each man bowed under pack,

helmet, ammunition, weapons, and entrenching tools, to board landing craft that bobbed alongside the big ships. The landing boats raced through the surf. Amtracs lumbered over reef and shoal and wallowed into shallow water with treads clanking.

Leathernecks spilled out of the craft and vaulted off amtracs; onto the beach they charged in skirmish formation. They moved with a skill acquired only by combat veterans. Most of the men had seen action on Guadalcanal; they were hard and fit for battle. The 2nd Marine Division was the best trained and equipped unit the United States had thrown into an amphibious operation up to that time.

Every man there knew that real landings did not go off so smoothly. This was only play-acting. No tracer bullets streaked out of hidden machine guns; no mortar shells exploded. There were no screaming wounded or shot-torn dead. The real test was yet to come for these sun-tanned, battle-toughened young Marines.

"Uncle" Julian Smith watched the performance of the landing rehearsals with less than avuncular pride from the deck of the *Maryland*. The general spotted numerous flaws and defects that a less expert military eye might have missed. The men were moving too slowly; some had bunched up on the beaches—a fatal error in combat; others dallied getting off the landing craft.

"I want speed, speed, and more speed! We have to hit the Nip while he's still groggy from our naval bombardment.

Speed will save lives and assure our victory in short order," General Smith said.

All things considered, the first phases of Operation Galvanic seemed to be going favorably. The Task Force had assembled on time, ships were being refueled according to schedule, and the men's morale was high.

But not everything went without a hitch. Colonel William Marshall, CO 2nd Marines, the spearhead regiment, was taken ill with a fever and had to be replaced. In his stead, Julian Smith picked Colonel David Shoup, the division operations officer.

Squat, red-faced Shoup was keenly aware of the responsibility that had fallen on him. As CO of the spearhead regiment, he would have to make decisions upon which hung the lives of his men and, possibly, the success of Operation Galvanic.

Few who heard Shoup's profane talk would have guessed that this thirty-nine-year-old career Marine was an honor graduate of De Pauw University. "Shoup sounded like a Marine noncom who had never finished eighth grade," noted a war correspondent with the division.

Exactly why Shoup had assumed the role of the traditional hard-boiled, semi-literate Leatherneck was a mystery. A fellow officer surmised: "It's my guess that Dave's trying to hide a gentle nature behind this 'tough guy' pose. However, I may be all wet. It's possible that he's exactly what he seems—a truly rough customer. Nobody really knows him."

Although Shoup's personality aroused speculation, Major General Julian Smith was bedeviled by matters more complex than his former operations officer's uncouth manner. The problem of Tarawa's coral reefs and wayward tides cropped up again and again; the reef and the tides were never out of his thoughts.

What if the worst happened on D-Day and there was no water to cover the fringing reef? In that case, 100 amtracs would not be enough to carry all the assault waves to the beaches. Defeat and disaster hinged on the unpredictable whims of the tide. . . .

At a staff meeting held Friday, November 12, aboard the *Maryland,* Julian Smith suggested that the invasion be postponed until November 22 when spring tides were due at Betio. But spring tides were always accompanied by strong westerly winds which kicked up a choppy sea with waves too high for launching landing craft. Also the five- to ten-foot-deep spring tide had been known to cover the beaches, thus leaving no place for the Marines to land.

"We had to make the best of a rotten situation," stated a 2nd Marine Division staff officer. "If neap tide gave us a headache, so did spring tide. Anyway, there was no chance of putting off D-Day. The machinery was in motion; ships, planes, men, and equipment were on the way. We had to move according to plan and there was no alternative."

"Uncle" Julian still fretted about his men crossing the

reef. "We have only enough amtracs to take in the first three waves. How do we put the rest of the troops ashore?"

No one could answer that question, but officers of battleships and cruisers sought to reassure him. "I predict that between carrier plane bombings and naval bombardment, the enemy will be wiped out before the first Leatherneck steps ashore," a cruiser's gunnery officer remarked.

"We'll bombard at 6,000 yards," a battleship captain announced. "We have so much armor that Tojo can't hurt us."

"We'll hit the Nips from 4,000 yards. Our armor can take the best the enemy will throw at us," the skipper of a cruiser said.

"Uncle" Julian listened to them, and then rose with grave dignity. The lamplight glinted off his silver-framed eyeglasses. "Gentlemen, I am most impressed by what you have said. But please remember one thing: When my boys land and meet the enemy at bayonet point, the only armor they'll have is the thickness of a Marine's government-issue shirt!"

CHAPTER THREE

BETIO

SATURDAY, NOVEMBER 20, 1943

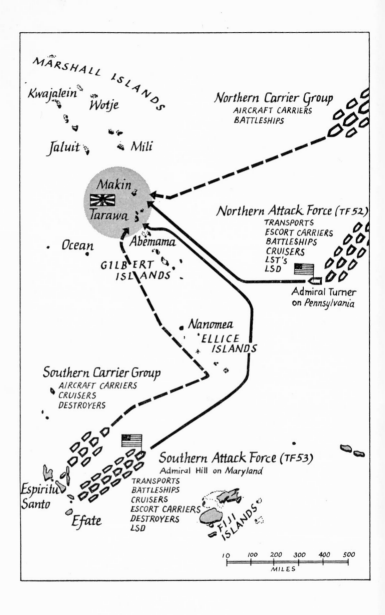

THREE

 1

From daybreak until dusk of Saturday, November 13, the 2nd Marine Division boarded the transports anchored in Efate's splendid harbor. All that day boats shuttled from shore to ship taking men out to the APA's. By sundown, the embarkation was completed. A signal blinked on the bridge of the transport *Monrovia,* flagship of the task force transport group.

"All ships sortie!" the message read.

One by one, the vessels swung into line and followed the *Monrovia* out to sea. At the harbor entrance, escorting destroyers and cruisers fell in around the transports. Task Force 53 was on the move, the majestic battleships attended by their cruisers and "tin cans."

Farther off steamed the task force's air support, Rear Admiral Alfred E. Montgomery's flattops: *Essex, Bunker Hill,* and *Independence,* backed up by ships of Cruiser Division (CRUDIV) 5: *Chester, Pensacola, Salt Lake City,* and the light cruiser *Oakland.* Swift destroyers darted vigilantly at the flanks of carriers and cruisers. Admiral Hill signaled the task force to take a northerly course, toward Tarawa Atoll and the rendezvous with destiny on Betio's landing beaches.

The voyage to Tarawa was long, hot, and boring. The ships followed a roundabout route to throw off any possible Japanese surveillance. Blinker lights flashed from the signal deck of the *Maryland,* which flew the flag of the task force commander, Rear Admiral Harry W. Hill. The flagship's messages were passed on from ship to ship by wigwag and lights since strict radio silence was enforced.

Hill tried to keep his sailors busy. He ordered cruisers and destroyers to hold daily battle practice. The battlewagons *Maryland, Tennessee,* and *Colorado* engaged in mock firing runs, while destroyers darted about laying simulated smoke screens and chasing imaginary subs. Cargo and transport vessels rehearsed emergency turns and other evasive tactics.

About 175 miles to the north of the main task force, carriers launched and recovered planes which flew antisubmarine patrols and scoured the skies for enemy aircraft. But not a single Japanese plane or submarine was seen during the week-long voyage. However, the hours spent in training operations were not wasted. Task Force 53 neared Tarawa with the ships' crews eager and alert, ready for the ordeal of battle.

The men who would do the actual fighting on Betio passed the sweltering days before combat as had warriors since time immemorial. They cleaned rifles and machine guns and honed knives and bayonets to razor sharpness. Some Marines passed the time sleeping on deck, in their bunks, or in any shady spot that could be found. Many played cards: poker, red dog, gin rummy, acey deucey, and black jack. The games were marathons of endurance. Hour after hour, days on end, the players shuffled, reshuffled, and dealt the pasteboards; the pots often reached monumental proportions. On one transport, a Marine private won $6,000 at poker.

That night he walked about the ship giving away money. When a buddy tried to stop him, he said, "Look, Mac, you can't take it with you; and, chances are, where we're going I won't need money. If I come through and live to be very old, I'll always remember the time I gave away six thousand bucks. A guy doesn't often get the chance to be a big shot, to feel like a millionaire."

Another favorite pastime of the Marines was letter writing. They wrote and wrote—to sweethearts, wives, mothers, fathers, relatives, and friends—neither knowing nor even caring when or if the letters would ever be mailed. It was a way to forget what they had to face.

The Marines were prodigious readers of any and all

printed matter. "You read what you could get your hands on: mysteries, old magazines, books—even training manuals. Just to read and keep your mind off the battle," a Marine remembered.

Mostly, the Leathernecks engaged in the Corps' most popular activity—griping and grousing. They grumbled about everything from the stench and heat below decks to the food. They bitterly criticized General Smith, their officers, noncoms, and each other. President and Mrs. Roosevelt received their share of verbal abuse, as did Churchill, Mussolini, Stalin, Hitler, Tojo, the Emperor of Japan, and the Brooklyn Dodgers.

The more carping and complaining they heard, the more the officers and noncoms smiled. "A man's no Marine unless he's sounding off about how crummy things are," a grizzled sergeant explained. "That's how you can tell when the boys are ready. Give me squawking troops every time. You're in trouble when they're moody and thoughtful. A guy shouldn't think too much before a battle. . . ."

Each day, for an hour or longer, the troops on every transport were briefed about the coming action; again and again they heard the part each unit would play. Battalions were always referred to as Red, White, or Blue. The 2nd (White) Battalion, 8th Marines, commanded by Major H. P. "Jim" Crowe, was to attack on the left, or eastern, flank (Beach Red 3). The 2nd (White) Battalion, 2nd Marines, under Lieutenant Colonel Herbert Amey, would hit in the

50

center (Beach Red 2). On the right, or western, flank would be the 3rd (Blue) Battalion, 2nd Marines, under Major John F. Schoettel. Their target was designated Beach Red 1. All the landing beaches were on the northern (lagoon) side of Betio. The western shore, called Beach Green, was not to be initially invested.

The Marines stared at huge bas-relief maps of Betio until every hummock and landmark was familiar. "I know that damn place better than I do my own mug," a private told his squad leader.

The Leathernecks also were told about pre-invasion, softening-up bombings and bombardments by planes and ships. On D-Day minus four (November 16), land-based Liberators from Funafuti would start pounding Betio. Other Japanese fields within the range of B-24's would be heavily attacked to cripple enemy air support for Tarawa. From sunrise to sunset of D-Day minus three and D-Day minus two, carrier planes would concentrate on Betio; on D-Day minus one, cruisers and bombers from TF 53 would hit the islet.

The naval bombardment of Betio on D-Day, the Marines were informed, was to be the greatest concentration of explosives ever fired at a single objective. Within a four-hour period, TF 53 would fire more than 2,000 tons of shells ranging from 16-inch battleship projectiles weighing almost 1,000 pounds each to 50-pound shells from the 5-inch guns of the destroyers. In addition, carrier aircraft would drop another 900 tons of high explosives, while fighters strafed Betio's defenders with machine guns and aerial cannon.

During the late afternoon of D-Day minus one (November 19), a message was flashed throughout TF 53 from the *Maryland:* "It is not the Navy's intention to wreck Betio. We do not intend to destroy it. We will obliterate it from the face of the earth. . . ."

This extravagant claim was read to the Marines on the transports. The Leathernecks reacted with derision. "There were Bronx cheers, hoots, and catcalls," a crewman on the APA *Zeilin* recalled. "The pithiest comment of all came from a private who hollered, 'Oh yeah? Tell it to the Marines!' "

The Leathernecks were unimpressed because they had heard the same sort of talk before other actions against the Japanese. "No matter how many tons of shells and bombs are dropped, there's still going to be some Nips left when we hit the beach. They'll be dug in real deep, waiting for us like they were on Tulagi. It'll take bayonets, grenades, and flamethrowers to dig them out. Yeah—and plenty of blood, too," a Guadalcanal veteran predicted to a war correspondent.

"That's it, all right," a second Marine chimed in. "We'll have to wade in and try to kill Nips while they try to kill us, and whoever kills the most will win. That's war without rose-colored glasses. Anybody who has other ideas about it is all wet."

So the time passed as TF 53 plowed through a mirror-surfaced sea in unbroken sunshine. A crewman on the heavy cruiser *Portland* noted in his diary: "After the war, I'm coming back to these parts. . . . I've never seen anything that compares to the Pacific when the sunlight dances on the water. . . ."

≡≡≡ ‖‖‖‖‖ 2

At sunset on November 19, the weather turned uncomfortably hot, and the men crowded in the *Maryland*'s chartroom that night sweated profusely. The air was stifling. Admiral Harry Hill was present, as was Major General Julian Smith, accompanied by his Chief of Staff, Colonel Merritt "Red Mike" Edson of Guadalcanal fame; there were transport captains, gunnery officers, and artillery commanders jammed in the sweltering cabin. They pored over maps and photos of Betio, checking final details of the invasion, now only a few hours off.

Seldom was a military action so well supplied with accurate pictorial material of enemy campaign as was Operation Galvanic. The photos taken in mid-September by the *Lexington*'s planes had been supplemented a fortnight later when the submarine *Nautilus* scouted Tarawa with a camera fitted to her periscope. The sub had prowled the atoll's coastline for days, snapping hundreds of feet of film through her 'scope. She also had reconnoitered Makin and Abemama.

The *Nautilus'* pictures plus the aerial photos gave almost total intelligence of the invasion beaches, the coastline, and the channel that led through the outer barrier reef into the lagoon. There now remained only the problem of putting the 2nd Marine Division ashore.

"Uncle" Julian Smith still worried about the fringing reef. He voiced his doubts to Colonel Edson. "Mike, I'm afraid we'll get hung up on the coral and take heavy casualties."

"I'm praying you're wrong, sir," "Red Mike" said, "but I have a hunch you're not. Tomorrow's going to be a long, ugly day."

At 2100 (9:00 P.M.) Admiral Hill rose from his chair at the chart table and faced the assembled officers. "Gentlemen, the time for discussion is over. We must now prepare to act. Good luck to you all." The meeting was over. The men filed out of the chartroom and separated to carry out their duties.

The warships proceeded to battle stations. Tampions (muzzle plugs) were removed from the guns. Armor-piercing (AP) shells were hauled up from the magazines. Gunnery officers checked fire-control communications; crews stood by in turrets. Signal lights flickered from one vessel to another as men stirred busily for the coming day's deadly work.

The Marines showed no sign of the tensions they must have been feeling. In crowded, steamy holds, leaders gave platoons final briefings. Weapons were cleaned for the last time. Each man received a day's K rations, two canteens filled with fresh water, and an extra bandolier of cartridges.

"Go easy on the water," a lieutenant advised his men. "We don't know how long it'll be before drinking water can be hauled ashore. The water you find on Betio may be polluted, so don't drink it!"

"Don't worry, sir. We won't get too thirsty. Not with all the *sake* those Nips always have around," a Leatherneck stated. (*Sake,* a rice wine, was highly favored by the Japanese, and supplies of it were kept with their troops.)

A submarine alarm sounded at 2200 (10:00 P.M.), when the destroyer *Ringgold,* running ahead of TF 53, picked up a radar blip that indicated a surfaced submarine in the area. Word was blinkered back to the flagship. Admiral Hill, fearing the intruder was an enemy patrol craft, ordered the *Ringgold* to open fire. The destroyer's first salvo hit the submarine, which quickly dived. Her damage control detail, working with swift efficiency, managed to save the "pig boat" (U.S. Navy slang for a submarine). An hour or two later, the underseas craft surfaced again and signaled the *Ringgold* that she was not Japanese but the faithful *Nautilus* coming to join the task force as ordered.

Apologies were proffered and accepted. Admiral Hill stated, "It's all my fault. I should have realized the sub was the *Nautilus.* I'm relieved the damage was slight and there were no casualties."

One pig boat man was not so easily mollified. He refused

to excuse the "bonehead" mistake. "Why, they might as well kill a guy as scare him to death. I'll bet those swabbies on the *Ringgold* wouldn't have come within a hundred yards of hitting us if we'd really been Japs!"

At one minute before midnight, lookouts on the cruiser *Santa Fe* sighted the Gilbert Islands from a position a few miles south of Tarawa. The armada swung northwest to the entry through Tarawa's barrier reef above Betio. The battleships, cruisers, and destroyers deployed to their firing stations. At 0045 (12:45 A.M.) Marine buglers on the troopships sounded reveille. At the first blast, the moon rose as if in response to the summons and roused much laughter. "I blow my brains out and can't stir up a Leatherneck, but the minute I sound off, the moon snaps to for me! Can you beat it?" a bugler asked.

Soon, Marines were astir, shuffling to transport galleys for a breakfast of scrambled eggs, steak, and coffee. After eating, the Leathernecks filed up on deck and formed into platoons. A freshening breeze cooled their sweat-drenched bodies. The men stood at ease, cracking gallows-humor jokes. A private called out, "Hey, Sarge! I owe you a pack of butts. . . ."

"So what?"

"So I'll give 'em to you now. I wouldn't want it on my conscience if you got knocked off. . . ."

The invasion fleet sailed up Tarawa's western shore to the lagoon entrance. At 0205 (2:05 A.M.) the channel was reached and about 45 minutes later lookouts sighted Betio. A short time after, the Marines aboard the transports could make out the island, a shadowy blob on the water.

"What's that out there?" a Leatherneck asked, pointing.

"The end of the line, Mac. Betio," someone replied.

"I sure wish it was Coney Island," a Brooklyn-accented voice rasped. . . .

≡|||||| 3

Once Betio hove into view, the transports jockeyed to launch Higgins Boats and amtracs. At 0355 (3:55 A.M.) the transport flagship *Monrovia* signaled "All ships ready for launching." Then the order "Boats away!" came from the *Maryland*. Soon a variety of small craft swarmed around the APA's. On board these vessels, loudspeakers squawked: "Marines, man your landing craft!" Over the side went the men clambering down nets to bobbing alligators and Higgins Boats.

The assault units mounted amtracs which fell into formation for the beach run. A variety of craft carrying reinforcements, artillery, and tanks lurched in the swell. When all shock troops were boated and attack lines formed a quarter of a mile off the lagoon entrance, the *Maryland* signaled, "This will be a glorious page in the history of the Marine Corps. God bless you all!"

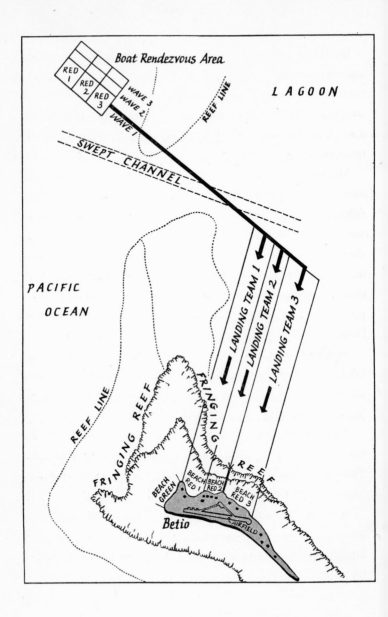

By 0430 (4:30 A.M.), the first assault wave was ready, and the amtracs moved up to the line of departure, some three miles north of Beaches Red 1, 2, and 3. The minesweepers, *Pursuit* and *Requisite,* dashed into the channel and cleared a lane through the mine field, dropping markers to show the safe corridor.

Marines, in green-mottled, cloth-covered steel helmets and green fatigues, crouching in pitching amtracs, clutching rifles, and ducking the spray that sloshed over the clumsy vessels' gunwales, wondered when the enemy would start shooting. So far, there had been no reaction from the Japanese. The foe's continued inactivity raised high the hope that he had given up without a fight and evacuated Betio, just as he had done on Kiska, in the Aleutians, when confronted by a powerful U.S.–Canadian invasion force.

Now, off Betio, it was whispered on every amtrac and landing craft, every transport and cargo ship, on battleships, cruisers, and destroyers, "Tojo's pulled another 'Kiska.' "

The rumor seemed logical enough. Surely the fleet's signal lights could be seen from Betio—if anyone was there. The silence must mean the Japanese had "taken a powder," "scrammed," "bugged out," as the sailors put it.

With each passing moment, this wishful thinking rose among the Americans. "Uncle" Julian Smith, on the *Maryland,* scanning Betio through night glasses, saw no movement on the islet.

"I prayed with all my might that this would be a second Kiska," he wrote later. But his fervent wish was not granted.

At 0441 (4:41 A.M.), everyone in the task force found out that the Japanese still occupied Betio.

A red star-shell cluster arched up from the south shore. Seconds after, several more meteor-like flares made parabolas through the night sky. Then complete darkness fell again and no further sign came from Betio. Now the silence throbbed with menace, not promise; the silence was an ominous blanket cloaking the movements of the wily foe. . . .

For some time Admiral Shibasaki had been aware of the invasion force's presence at the lagoon entrance. Sentries had spotted winking signal lights and informed the CP. The admiral withheld the order to open fire. Instead, he sent up flares to alert his defenses. Answering star shells told him his forces were ready. Shibasaki called the battery commanders by telephone and told them, "When you have a good target, fire at your own discretion. Make every shell count. Good shooting. Long live the Emperor! *Banzai!*"

For almost thirty minutes after the flares had sped skyward, nothing happened. The alligators plodded to the jump-off point. Higgins Boats and other beaching craft circled the transports. Every man stared at the shore, wondering when "the ball would begin."

At 0505 (5:05 A.M.) a Kingfisher (KOS2U) scout plane, piloted by Lieutenant Commander Robert MacPherson, was catapulted from the *Maryland*. The flier was to be the eyes for General Julian Smith and Admiral Harry Hill during the landings. Just after the Kingfisher buzzed off into a sky momentarily growing lighter to the east, a shore battery opened up on the flagship at a range of about 11,000 yards.

Shells splashed around the big battlewagon. From the bridge, Admiral Hill nodded permission for his staff gunnery officer to shoot back. The *Maryland* rocked as her 16-inchers roared and spat flame. Explosions sounded from shore when her shells landed. A second broadside bellowed.

On Betio a searing sheet of fire leaped almost 500 feet high. Ear-shattering detonations sent shock waves across the water. The boated Marines jumped up, cheering. Exultant yells rang from the American ships. One blast after another erupted ashore. It was learned after the battle that a single 16-inch AP shell had blown up an 8-inch battery's ammunition magazine; the hit set off tons of shells, wrecked the emplacement, and killed dozens of men.

While the *Maryland* poured her broadsides upon the islet, the big guns of the *Tennessee* and the *Colorado* joined the thunderous chorus. Heavy cruisers went to work with 8-inchers, light cruisers added their 6-inchers, and destroyers raced in close to rake the shoreline.

The air was filled with hundreds of *swooshing* shells. "They sound like fast freight trains overhead," noted a Marine in an amtrac.

"You couldn't see anything but black smoke and flames from one end of Betio to the other. I figured that's what Hell must be like," said a sailor on the *Tennessee*.

The noted war correspondent, Robert Sherrod, observed the bombardment from the deck of a transport. He wrote: "The whole island of Betio seemed to erupt with bright fires that were burning everywhere. They blazed even through the thick wall of smoke that curtained the island. . . ."

This punishment continued until 0542 (5:42 A.M.). Then Admiral Hill ordered a cease fire because Rear Admiral Montgomery's carriers were due to launch a strike at 0545 (5:45 A.M.). Dawn was breaking, and the fires on Betio stood out like crimson splotches against the grayish background. The silence that came when the American guns stopped was welcome after all the noise.

"We weren't used to the quiet and still shouted at the top of our voices as though everyone was stone deaf. It took a little time to realize we could speak in a normal manner," a *Maryland* gunner remembered.

Sailors and Marines craned at the sky, searching for the Avenger (TBF), Dauntless (SBD), Helldiver (SB2C), and Hellcat (F6F) planes to appear but no aircraft came. A ripple of anxiety went through the fleet. Where were the planes?

Minutes ticked off and the Marines in the alligators grumbled uneasily: "Damn those flyboys! They couldn't get out of bed on time."

"That's not it at all," a Leatherneck sneered. "They're too busy posing for the newsreel cameras."

After several more minutes, men began to shout in anger and frustration. They cursed bitterly at this apparent betrayal by the carrier planes. (Actually, the aircraft were winging toward Betio, late only because of a misunderstanding. Admiral Montgomery thought he was to hit Betio at sunrise which came at 0615 [6:15 A.M.]. However, Admiral Hill had requested that the planes arrive at dawn, a half hour before the sun came up.)

Suddenly the guns on Betio began to blaze away at transports, and shells splashed among the landing craft. The naval guns had not wiped out the enemy batteries as had been believed. Several salvos almost struck transports crowded with troops and Admiral Hill signaled the vessels to pull out of range.

The ships scuttled away with landing craft and amtracs tagging after them. Lieutenant Commander MacPherson, in the *Maryland*'s scout plane, noted: ". . . the transports reminded me of fat mother ducks followed by their broods. . . ."

Admiral Hill did not answer the shore batteries for about 20 minutes, since he still expected the planes. He waited until 0605 (6:05 A.M.), and then the flagship raised the signal: "Commence firing!" The armada opened up again and pummeled the Japanese for ten minutes until bombers and fighters from the *Essex, Bunker Hill,* and *Independence* were seen approaching in attack formation. The fliers reached the target area at 0615 (6:15 A.M.), the precise moment the sun climbed over the eastern horizon.

The ships held fire as dive-bombers screamed down and Hellcats strafed the foe. The Marines, who had so soundly cursed the airmen, now cheered them. Smoke and flame once more obscured Betio; the islet seemed to heave under the explosions. The planes wheeled and flew off after seven minutes; none had been hit by the feeble AA fire. No sooner had they departed than the ships commenced an even more violent bombardment.

As the cannonading progressed, Admiral Hill gradually closed in until battlewagons, cruisers, and tin cans were firing over open sights at almost pointblank range. All who saw the barrage thought nothing could withstand such a storm of high explosive. The men on ships, Higgins Boats, and amtracs recalled Admiral Hill's promise to "obliterate the island."

Apparently that promise was going to be kept.

The shelling went on for two and a half hours until nothing could be seen of Betio through the wall of smoke and dust. As the bombardment reached a crescendo, the *Pursuit* and the *Requisite* steamed through the channel and entered the lagoon, followed by the *Ringgold* and the *Dashiell*. Waddling in the wake of these two tin cans churned 100 amtracs, each carrying 20 to 25 Marines. The alligators were aligned in three ranks. Forty-eight were in the first wave, 24 in the second, and 28 made up the third.

Also moving up through the channel were Higgins Boats and various other types of landing craft, some with troops, some with vehicles, artillery, and supplies.

Smoke from the fires ashore enshrouded the Marines in the amtracs. They were self-confident to the point of cockiness. No previous amphibious landing had ever had such overwhelming naval support. The bombarding guns were described as "the voice of doom for the Japs. . . ."

"Their noise numbed a man's senses . . . explosions jarred you to the marrow . . . earth and sea trembled . . . ," a war correspondent noted.

The minesweepers and destroyers led the amtracs into the lagoon and headed for Betio. "The island was all ablaze. You couldn't see anything but fire and smoke. Every once in a while a great pillar of flame shot skyward as though a volcano had erupted. . . . A sailor standing near me gave a sickly grin. . . . 'Mate, they need firemen there, not Marines,' he said. And I thought, it's going to be a cinch for our guys . . . they'll find nothing but splintered palm trees and dead Japs . . . ," a *Ringgold* crewman wrote after the battle.

≡≡≡ ||||||| 4

The Japanese were not yet through. Somehow, a shore battery had survived the bombardment and shot at the ships in the lagoon. A dud shell tore through the *Ringgold*'s engine room and was followed by a second, which also failed to explode. "Lady Luck was riding with us," a machinist's mate commented.

The *Ringgold*'s gunnery officer spotted the flashes of the enemy cannon, and the destroyer's 5-inchers bracketed the annoying battery. A second salvo blasted the position, which disintegrated when a direct hit struck its ammunition dump.

No more shellfire came from Betio.

Admiral Hill ended the naval bombardment at 0855 (8:55 A.M.) because the amtracs were then so close to shore that he feared a short round might fall among them. However, the two destroyers and the two minesweepers in the lagoon kept up a steady drumfire on Beach Red 1. A flight of Hellcats swooped low and briefly strafed the landing areas.

From sea and lagoon Betio seemed devastated. Opinion on the *Maryland* was that the shelling had killed, wounded, or dazed the defenders.

That was only partly true. The Imperial Marines who had been caught in the open by the bombardment were either dead or disabled. But most of Betio's garrison still lived. The coconut-log bunkers and the pillboxes, covered by layers of concrete and sand, withstood the pounding of even the 16-inch shells.

The men in them had quivered and trembled under the pounding and the blasting, a few had cracked and lay huddled in corners whimpering like whipped dogs, but the majority of the disciplined Imperial Marines had "sweated out" the shelling.

A Japanese lieutenant gave this description of it in his diary, which was found after the battle:

> *The earth shook; the sky was a fiery ball. . . . I stayed with my men at our machine guns in a bunker which covered a field of fire on the western lagoon side beach. . . . I thought of my family as shells slammed around us . . . we were flung about like rag dolls by the explosions. . . . I thought of honor and courage and the Mikado. . . . We had taken an oath to give our lives for the Son of Heaven . . . and this was the acid test. . . . I told my men we must not fail or we would dishonor the Emperor, our country and our ancestors . . . and so we endured. . . .*

Despite the furious American cannonading, the island's defense system was not destroyed. Only those installations above ground suffered. Communications lines were severed, radio equipment smashed. All AA guns had been knocked out and the coastal batteries silenced. Hardly a vehicle remained intact. Barracks, storehouses, and sheds had been set ablaze.

At the airfield, hangars, repair shops, and the control tower were destroyed. But machine-gun nests, rifle pits, pillboxes, bunkers, and blockhouses stood almost unscathed. (A study by ordnance experts made some time later proved that close-range naval gunfire was ineffective against targets such as those on Betio. One-ton aerial bombs, rockets, and heavy mortars would have done more damage than the battleships.)

When the bombardment ceased, Admiral Shibasaki tried to reach his scattered units by telephone from his mammoth command post bunker, but all the lines were down. Radios were inoperative. The admiral was cut off from those of his men who had survived. The only troops he controlled were the 300 picked Imperial Marines who manned the CP.

Shibasaki intended to fight even if Yankee shells had killed everyone else on Betio. He knew each man in the CP preferred death to surrender. A breeze cleared away the smoke that veiled the beaches from the bunker's observation post. An officer peered out through binoculars. He lowered the glasses and cried, "Admiral! The Americans . . . !"

Shibasaki took the proffered glasses. He saw amtracs

plowing steadily to the beach. His anti-boat guns would have a fine time shooting at those slow-moving targets. And he saw, too, jagged points of the coral fringing reef jutting out of the water. The tide had not failed him; the Yankees would not be able to cross the reef in boats. They would have to wade through the surf. Oh, if only enough of his machine gunners were still alive to mow them down.

Sweeping the beach with the binoculars he could find nothing to reassure him; only truncated trees, gaping shell holes, and splintered debris. Smoke spiraled upward, and flames danced over a torn and tortured wasteland. A freighter, the *Saida Maru,* lay on her side near the Burns Philp pier. A destroyer's guns had bowled her over.

On the beach and by the seawall, Shibasaki made out the crumpled corpses of men killed by the gunfire. Disheartened, the admiral was about to turn away—there would be no anti-boat guns to sink the Yankees. His men had been slaughtered. What was left to do but lead the CP troops in a *banzai* charge as the Yankees pushed ashore?

Then a movement caught his eye. A small Rising Sun signal flag had been poked out of a pillbox's firing slit. It waved frantically. Then, at different points, more, and still more, flags appeared from rifle pits, machine-gun positions, pillboxes, and bunkers. Here, one was seen at an anti-boat gun emplacement; there, at a mortar post. Dozens of them fluttered defiantly. The tiny flags meant his men lived; this meant many Yankees would die.

69

Shibasaki smiled tightly and focused on the American boats. Clumsy, waddling monsters, so neatly aligned, each trailing frothy wake as it bucked and plunged up to the reef. The admiral gasped when the amtracs climbed out of the water, crawled across the reef, and plunged into the lagoon again.

He had never seen anything like that before! Ah, well. The insolent American dogs! They were clever. But cleverness was not enough. Now, they would feel the wrath of the Samurai. The Yankees would find only shallow graves on Betio!

5

The Marines of the 2nd Division agreed that the ruggedest, toughest Leathernecks in the outfit were the 34 men who made up the Scout-Sniper (S&S) Platoon which was commanded by First Lieutenant William Deane Hawkins, known as "The Hawk."

Every man in the S&S was deadly with rifle, tommy gun, pistol, grenade, and knife. Besides that, each knew how to use explosives and was a judo expert. One needed the instinct of a tiger and the skill of an Apache in the S&S.

"The Hawk" led a band of steel-nerved fighters who feared nothing. They never used their CO's real name. To them, he was "The Hawk." The tall, lean officer actually resembled that fierce bird. His face was sharp featured, with hard black eyes that missed nothing. He had deep pride in the Marine Corps and absolute confidence in his platoon.

"We can lick any 200-man company," twenty-nine-year-old Hawkins said with assurance.

The S&S CO fatalistically believed he was destined to die in battle. When he had joined the Marines, shortly after the attack on Pearl Harbor, Hawkins told his best friend, "Mac, I'll see you someday—but not on this earth."

"The Hawk" had a philosophy about war: "I think war is wicked and rotten—but if war comes a man must face it without flinching. You have to die anyway, but if you die for your country, your death has some meaning."

"The Hawk" had fought so well on Guadalcanal that he was given a battlefield commission as a second lieutenant. He soon rose a grade, and the command of the S&S platoon fell to him. This outfit got the toughest job of the invasion. They were to hit the beach ahead of the first wave and seize the Burns Philp pier. Intelligence believed the foe had riflemen and machine gunners hidden among the pilings and in the sheds that lined the pier.

The S&S rode ahead of the shock troops in an amtrac that reached the fringing reef just before 0900 (9:00 A.M.). All the way across the outer lagoon not a shot had been fired from shore, but when the alligator started climbing the reef, gears grinding and treads clanking, mortar shells began raining on all sides. An anti-boat (AB) gun let loose with a near-miss, and machine-gun bullets rattled off the amtrac's armor as the vehicle jounced across the reef and slid into the shallow water on the opposite side.

Rifle bullets whistled close or ricocheted off. The amtrac's twin .50's returned the fire until the gunner dropped, shot through the heart. "The Hawk" leaped up and took his place, spraying the pier with twin streams of lead.

The amtrac scraped on the beach and the S&S platoon vaulted out. One squad, led by "The Hawk," raced to the seawall and jumped over it without losing a man. Demolitionists, carrying TNT charges and flame throwers, followed Lieutenant Alan Leslie to the pier. Bullets kicked up sand. Grenades *whumped*. The battle was joined. Shrapnel

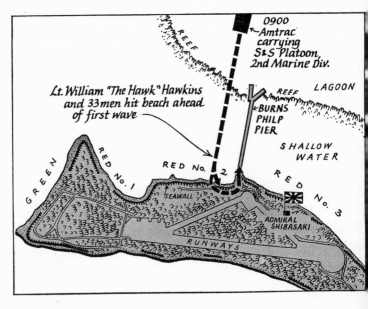

from a mortar shell hit "The Hawk" in the back. His fatigue coat was drenched with blood.

"Hey, Lieutenant! You need a medic!" a Marine shouted.

"Medic, hell! I'm not here for a health cure! I came to fight!" "The Hawk" cried, hurling grenades at a machine-gun nest.

Unearthly shrieks rose from beneath the pier as a spurt of fiery liquid from Lieutenant Leslie's flame throwers caught three riflemen hidden there. Wreathed in flames, the Japanese tumbled into the water. The old timber of the pier also began to burn.

While this was going on, the amtracs, with men of the 2nd (White) Battalion, 8th Marines, under Major Henry P. Crowe, touched Beach Red 3. A fusillade from machine guns and rifles spattered among the Leathernecks as they darted for the seawall. A dozen fell, dead or wounded. Major Crowe, a red-mustachioed giant, waved his men on to the wall. Some tried to go over and were mowed down; the rest leaped into shell holes and took cover. The attack stalled, and White Battalion was jammed onto a narrow stretch of sand swept by rifles, machine guns, and mortars. Demolition men crawled forward to find the weapons that raked them.

AB guns opened up as the amtracs turned and headed back for the reef. One alligator caught a direct hit and exploded. A second, riddled by shrapnel, turned turtle and sank. Several more blew up. The water was dotted with the corpses of Marines drifting on the surface. Cries were heard for corpsmen as the wounded called for help. Ignoring bullets and shrapnel, medics splashed out to their aid and dragged the injured men ashore.

At Beach Red 2, White Battalion, 2nd Marines, commanded by Lieutenant Colonel Herbert Amey, was also taken to shore in amtracs. The craft carrying Amey was disabled and started sinking about 30 yards offshore.

"Follow me!" the CO shouted, and leaped into a few feet of water. An instant later he fell, shot through the head. His men splashed past him to the beach. The other amtracs in that wave lurched upon land, where shells and incendiary bullets set most of them afire.

The Marines of Blue Battalion, 2nd Regiment (Major John F. Schoettel), were badly mauled as they attempted to make Beach Red 1. The enemy's defenses there had been only slightly damaged by the naval bombardment. The Imperial Marines waited in coconut-log revetments until the Leathernecks were less than 100 yards from shore. Then the Japanese unleashed a blizzard of high explosives and bullets.

Almost all the amtrac drivers were killed and the vehicles wallowed helplessly until volunteers took the controls. Three amtracs blew up, killing the men they carried

Others, holed by shells, went down. The men wading in the surf offered easy targets for enemy riflemen. A private who survived that ghastly trek to shore later wrote:

> *They were knocking out boats left and right. A tractor'd get hit, stop, and burst into flames, with men jumping out like torches. . . .*
>
> *Guys were sprawled all over the place. I looked across at my buddy who was only five feet from me. He was on his back and his face was all bloody. . . .*
>
> *Our boat was stopped, and they were laying lead to us from a pillbox. . . . Everybody seemed stunned, so I yelled, "Let's get the hell outa here!" I grabbed my carbine and an ammunition box . . . and . . . rolled over into the water. . . . Only about a dozen of the twenty-five went over the side with me, and only about four of us ever got ashore.*

Resistance on Beach Red 1 was so severe that only two companies, under Major Mike Ryan, actually landed. Major John Schoettel, the battalion CO, was unable to come in with the rest of the men. His amtracs had been slowed up by an unexpected reef on the right flank of Beach Red 1, and intensive fire from the Japanese kept them from climbing it. Schoettel tried gamely to land, time after time, until most of his amtracs had been sunk or badly damaged.

75

The water was filled with men floundering toward the blazing beach. The desperate major radioed assault-commander Colonel David Shoup, who was then aboard the *Monrovia:*

"Unable to land. Receiving heavy fire along the beach. Issue in doubt," Schoettel said.

"Land on Beach Red 2 and work west," Shoup ordered.

"We have nothing left to land," came the grim response a short time later.

≡ |||||| 6

An hour after the first troops reached shore, they had made virtually no progress inland. Crowe's men clung to a front about 200 yards wide, but only some 20 yards deep, on Beach Red 2; on Beach Red 3 Colonel Amey's men were pinned to a narrrow strip of sand. Lieutenant Colonel Walter Irvine Jordan, the highest-ranking officer present, an observer from the 4th Marine Division, took over the decimated battalion. He managed to lead the survivors of one company about 100 yards inland through a gap in the seawall. That was the farthest penetration made by the Americans. But Jordan and his men were in a bad spot. Losses were high, and the position they held was precarious. Jordan radioed Colonel Shoup: "We need help. Situation bad."

By this time, Shoup had come ashore and established a command post (CP) west of the pier. His own plight was critical and he had no help to send. The CO had landed after many difficulties and suffered a painful wound in his right thigh from a mortar-shell splinter. Shoup refused to be evacuated. With a blood-stained bandage around his leg, he remained on the beach trying to reorganize his shattered troops. Aiding him were Lieutenant Colonel Evans P. Carlson and several other staff officers.

The divisional CP was set up near a smashed Japanese bunker. The Marines had cornered some Japanese in there and Shoup posted sentries at the bunker mouth. He gave them orders to "kill the first Nip who shows his face. . . ."

The landing beaches were a welter of confusion. There was wild fighting on every side. Marines attacked pillboxes with grenades, TNT, and flamethrowers. At one place, a sniper concealed behind a pile of coconut logs killed two Marines in succession from a distance of only 30 yards.

He was detected by a flamethrower operator who squirted the hiding place with a stream of fiery liquid. The logs lit up with a roar. The sniper staggered out with his clothing afire. He staggered a few steps and then fell. The flames set off the cartridges in his belt and bullets popped. "We all hit the deck. Nobody wanted to get knocked off by a dead Nip," a Marine said.

The Japanese pounded the Americans with artillery from the eastern end of Betio. Colonel Shoup radioed for all the fire support he could get. The battleship *Tennessee* and two destroyers raced up to plaster the enemy guns while Hellcats strafed them. In a short time the enemy artillery was silenced.

Acts of incredible heroism took place as Leathernecks attempted to push off the beach. They advanced in groups of twos and threes over the seawall and disappeared into the smoke and dust cloud that hung over Betio. Some men had to fight alone. One such was Staff Sergeant Bill Bordelon whose amtrac had been torn apart by anti-boat gun shells at a range of 500 yards. Only Bordelon and three privates of the 25 men aboard survived the explosion. The three Leathernecks followed the sergeant as he waded toward land. Bordelon was lugging a pack full of TNT satchel charges. He came out of the water without the others. They had been shot dead.

Bordelon spied a machine-gun muzzle protruding from a firing slit in the seawall. He set a satchel charge and, leaping over the inert bodies of fallen Marines, hurled the TNT block. The Japanese position vanished in a blinding flash. The sergeant primed a second charge and crawled within throwing distance of another machine gun which he blasted. As he knocked out a third nest, a sniper wounded him in the chest. The rugged noncom killed the assailant with his carbine.

A wounded man called from the surf for help. Bleeding profusely, Bordelon dragged the Leatherneck to shore. He waved off a corpsman who wanted to treat his chest wound.

"Take care of that man," Bordelon ordered, pointing to the Marine he had rescued.

Perhaps, at that moment, he sensed his own wound was a fatal one, and that nothing could save him. Though his life was ebbing, Bordelon still had fight left. He lurched toward a pillbox and, with his last strength, threw a TNT pack into the firing slit. As the charge went off, Bill Bordelon crumpled to the sand and died.

Meanwhile, men of the fourth, fifth, and sixth landing waves were waiting beyond the fringing reef in Higgins Boats for amtracs to shuttle them ashore. Many of the amtracs that had carried the first three waves were either sunk or damaged; a ghastly toll had been taken of their drivers, gunners, and crews.

Fifteen amtracs, riddled by bullets and shell splinters, foundered after leaving the beach. The surviving amtracs drifted aimlessly about the lagoon. Many had no crewmen left. Major Henry Drewes, CO of the amtrac battalion, was dead.

First (Red) Battalion, 2nd Marines (Major Wood R. Kyle), waded into Beach Red 2 taking terrible losses on the way. Third (Blue) Battalion, 8th Marines (Major Robert H. Ruud), had been ordered to Beach Red 3. Finding no amtracs to take them in, Blue Battalion began the arduous march through the water to the beach—more than 700 yards away—where Crowe's hard-pressed troops sorely needed reinforcement.

The foe's machine gunners were merciless. They sprayed Ruud's men with bullets until the gun barrels glowed red. In addition to this murderous fire, machine guns chattered from the hulk of the *Saida Maru*. Daring Japanese had swum out to the wreck with automatic weapons. Individual Imperial Marines sneaked onto abandoned amtracs and turned those guns on the wading Leathernecks from the rear.

Marines fell one after another, under that withering fire. A sailor on the *Dashiell* watched the battalion's agony through his binoculars. "It was like a war movie. Those poor guys plodding in chest-high water and getting shot down. I tried not to look, but I couldn't turn away. The horror of it hypnotized me. If I get to be a hundred years old I'll always remember the slaughter of Blue Battalion, Eighth Marines," he commented later.

Lieutenant Commander MacPherson stared down at the tiny figures in the lagoon from the *Maryland*'s Kingfisher plane. He recalled: "The water was dotted with men advancing a step at a time, as though in slow motion. . . . They kept falling, falling, falling . . . singly, in groups, and in rows. . . . Higgins Boats brought more and more of them to the reef and they ran out and then began that long walk. . . . I wept tears of grief for the dead and of anger that I was unable to have helped them. . . ."

The exhausted survivors of Blue Battalion finally staggered ashore on Beach Red 3. A Leatherneck who had landed with the first wave at the outset of the invasion eyed the bedraggled newcomers staggering ashore. The battle-weary Marine shook his head sadly. "They call those rein-forcements? Those sad sacks are in worse shape than we are," he said to a buddy.

The Americans were in trouble all along the beach, and word flashed back to the ships: "Condition critical. The outcome is in doubt." One radio message, sent from an unidentified source, stated: "Have landed. Heavy opposi-tion. Casualties 70 percent. We've had it. Can't hold. We're licked."

In the chartroom of the *Maryland* a staff officer turned to his aide and hoarsely whispered, "Perhaps God may someday forgive us for having sent those boys to certain death. . . ."

≡ ||||||| 7

Although the Marines absorbed frightful punishment, the Japanese also suffered. The S&S platoon had ranged deep into the foe's defenses and killed ten times their own num-bers. "The Hawk's" men shot snipers out of trees, demol-ished machine-gun nests, and knifed and bayoneted Shiba-saki's soldiers in their foxholes. The Japanese did not know where the deadly Leathernecks would strike next. "The Hawk" was the ace killer among them. "I saw 'The Hawk' carrying a tommy gun. He had grenades dangling from his belt. He was still bleeding from his wounds but nothing could stop him. . . . I'll bet he racked up fifty Nips single-handed," a Marine officer reminisced.

The Americans eked out other successes besides those won by the S&S platoon. Over on Beach Red 1 (the western flank of the islet) Major Mike Ryan had reorganized his two companies—King (K) and Love (L). After gaining a toehold on Beach Red 1, Ryan's Marines attacked toward the sector marked Beach Green on the maps. Although Major Schoettel and the rest of Blue Battalion were still unable to land because of formidable resistance in the center of Beach Red 1, King and Love companies slugged toe-to-toe with the enemy.

Ryan received welcome and unexpected help. Sherman tanks had been brought to the reef in an LCT (Landing Craft, Tank) and the armored vehicles were unloaded there. They drove across the coral barrier into water three feet deep. The Shermans splashed and snorted ahead like prehistoric monsters, and crawled onto the beaches.

Once ashore they attacked machine-gun nests and pillboxes, but, within an hour or two, almost all had been put out of commission—especially on Beach Red 2 and Beach Red 3. (Only one tank—*Colorado*—remained in the fray at Beach Red 3, Major Crowe's sector—and none was left in workable condition at Beach Red 2, Lieutenant Colonel Jordan's zone.)

Six tanks had been allotted to Ryan's sector. Of these,

four were knocked out in the water. The remaining two Shermans joined King and Love companies' attack along the western flank. One of them, *China Gal,* commanded by Lieutenant Edward Bales, fought a head-on duel with a Japanese light tank. The enemy scored first, but its 37-mm shell barely dented *China Gal's* tough hide. Then the Sherman's 75-mm cannon slammed a shell through the foe's thin armor. The magazine was ignited and the Japanese vehicle exploded.

A Dauntless (SBD) bomber, sent to support Major Crowe's embattled White Battalion, 8th Marines, on Beach Red 3, unwittingly destroyed a Sherman. The SBD peeled off in a vertical dive and dropped a bomb squarely on a Japanese ammunition dump. The spectacular explosion rocked the islet like an earthquake tremor. Unfortunately, the tank happened to be passing the dump at the moment the bomb fell and was blown to pieces. The luckless battalion had just launched an attack when the bomb struck. The barrage of artillery shells and small-arms ammunition that came from the shattered dump broke up the American onslaught, and the Marines dived for cover.

With bullets whining past and shrapnel whirling nastily through the air, a Marine rose to one knee and shook his fist at the homeward bound Dauntless.

"You lousy flyboy! You must be working for Tojo!" the angry Leatherneck shouted.

"Yeah, with friends like him, who needs enemies?" another Marine laughed hollowly.

Once the ammunition stopped exploding, Crowe ordered the attackers forward again. Progress was slow and costly; the Japanese fought tenaciously. The foe quickly accounted for two of White Battalion's four tanks with antitank guns. The SBD had destroyed a third; but the fourth tank, the *Colorado,* commanded by Lieutenant Lou Largey, had a charmed life. The tank survived a direct hit from an antitank missile, a hail of grenades and Molotov cocktails, and a land mine. She was fire-blackened, dented, and battered; her crew was bruised, cut, and weary. But they kept going. The tank was the terror of the Beach Red 3 sector, riding over foxholes, blasting pillboxes, and killing Japanese.

Admiral Shibasaki, also, put some armor in action. Two light tanks, that somehow had lived through the monstrous naval bombardment of the morning, clattered across the island from the southern shore to counterattack Crowe. At the same time, the Americans were dragging a 37-mm antitank gun onto the beach. The boat that carried the 900-pound cannon had been sunk, but the gunners hand-hauled the heavy-wheeled piece through the water.

The Japanese tanks sped to the beach with machine guns spitting. The only weapon powerful enough to stop them was the 37-mm cannon gun, but to shoot at the tanks it had to be positioned atop the seawall.

Ordinarily, a block-and-tackle would have been required

to hoist up the gun. Faced by two oncoming hostile tanks, the Leathernecks in their path performed prodigies. "Lift the gun!" a sergeant bellowed. "Lift the damned thing onto the wall!"

"We grabbed hold of that cannon and literally threw it up there," a Tarawa veteran remembered.

The cannon's first round hit the leading tank, which spun around and burst into flames. The next shell scored on the second tank. Smoke billowed from the vehicle. The hatch cover opened, and the crew piled out. Marines called for them to surrender, but the Japanese tried to flee and were shot in their tracks.

As the battle raged across Betio, the medics displayed unbelievable courage caring for the many wounded. Because the beachhead was narrow, doctors and corpsmen had to work under fire. Red Cross flags, planted on the beaches, marked aid stations. Heedless of bullets and shells, the corpsmen patched up hundreds of torn and bleeding men; emergency operations were performed right on the beach. Rifles thrust in the sand supported bottles of plasma. But there were too few medics and too many wounded.

There were wounded men in the water, on the reef, clinging to the smoldering pier, lying in half-sunk amtracs; men whose life's blood flowed out through gaping tears and jagged slashes. Stretcher bearers hunted for them but missed scores. Some men had to face pain and death alone;

no one heard their fading cries for help. A single voice calling out was lost in the battle's din, and men who might have been saved died without even a word or a prayer to comfort them.

The Red Cross flags caught the eye of Japanese infiltrators. The rows of wounded lying bunched together made easy targets for grenades, and Shibasaki's men sneaked back to the beaches. They swam in from the *Saida Maru* and the wrecked amtracs. They crept up from demolished pillboxes. Carrying no weapons but a few hand grenades, each was aware that he was on a suicide mission. There would be little chance to get away. Yankee Marines with tommy guns and bayoneted rifles guarded the medics and the wounded.

Veterans of Guadalcanal knew all about infiltrators. They also knew the enemy had no scruples against killing wounded men. "Maybe the Nips were more honest than we were. War is murder, so what does it matter if you murder the wounded? Didn't we drop bombs on civilians? Does a wounded soldier deserve more mercy than a kid in a city far behind the lines? I guess that's how the Nips felt. So did we, but none of us ever said it aloud," a combat Marine stated years later.

The Japanese launched many attempts at the aid stations but failed every time. Of all the infiltrators, only one actually came within grenade-throwing distance. He was tall for a Japanese and his features were of Caucasian cast. At a casual glance he could have passed for one of the Americans. Disguised in U.S. Marine fatigues and helmet he strode into the Beach Red 2 sector. There was a crowded aid station about fifty yards east of the pier.

No one noticed the "Leatherneck" walking toward the Red Cross flag. The doctors and corpsmen were busy tending the scores of wounded. The infiltrator stopped about 20 yards from a cluster of stretchers filled with groaning men. He was reaching under his jacket for a grenade when a sentry standing near by shouted a warning and shot him down with a burst of tommy-gun fire. Marines came running up. A corporal grabbed the sentry.

"Are you nuts? You killed a Marine!" the noncom shouted.

"No! He's a *Jap!* I tell you he's a *Jap!*" the sentry insisted. "Look at his feet!"

The dead man was wearing *zoori*—canvas shoes specially designed for the Japanese army. The corporal released the sentry. "Yeah. Good work, Mac. Pretty sharp the way you spotted him."

A Leatherneck stared at the dead man. "He thought of everything—uniform, everything—and he'd have made it, too, except for the shoes."

"That's right," the sentry said. "If he'd have been wearing Marine Corps boondockers, I'd never have spotted him. That Nip had guts to try it. *Real* guts." The Leatherneck shook his head.

As the fighting continued, it became obvious that the wounded had to be taken off Betio and brought back to the ships. There was neither room nor facilities for them on shore. Since landing craft could not come in to pick up the wounded, a system for evacuating them was improvised. After a man had been given emergency treatment, he was put in a rubber boat with as many others as the craft could carry. A corpsman then waded out to the reef towing the laden rubber boat after him. At the reef, the wounded men were transferred to launches and landing craft for the trip out to the fleet.

It was slow and dangerous work. Mortars and machine guns raked the coral barrier. Shells exploded on the reef and caused additional casualties. One shell exploded in a Higgins Boat loaded with wounded and killed everyone aboard. The waters around the reef were filled with dead Marines.

More than 30 wrecked amtracs with bodies littered the barrier. Yet the task of getting the wounded to the ships went on.

The medics worked with dedication and devotion; they never flinched or hesitated under fire, but, like all Marines, kept grumbling, complaining, and griping, often with bitter humor, about the ordeal they were going through.

One corpsman stayed on his feet when a nearby mortar burst caused everyone else to dive prone. "Hit the dirt, Doc!" a Marine yelled at the medic.

"Why? If I get killed, my troubles are over. If I'm lucky and catch a stateside wound, they'll ship me home. And I'll be a war hero and sell bonds to rich civilians. So why should I duck?" the medic said.

"Gee, maybe you have something there," answered the Marine, standing up alongside the corpsman. . . .

≣ ‖‖‖‖ 8

Colonel David Shoup, limping badly, paced the narrow confines of his makeshift CP as he tried to direct his forces in battle. By afternoon some 5,000 Marines were ashore, but almost 1,500 of them were dead or wounded.

Out beyond the fringing reef milled boatloads of reinforcements, unable to land because there were no amtracs to take them across the reef. Officers were reluctant to order another wade-in after the decimation of Blue Battalion, 8th Marines. Farther out in the lagoon, cargo ships were loading landing craft with supplies, rations, ammunition, bulldozers, tools, clothing, tents, spare parts, wire, kitchen equipment, and a thousand other items needed ashore.

The boats circled about, creating a maritime traffic jam that reminded one New Yorker of "Times Square on New Year's Eve." None of the supply-carrying boats could get to the beaches and, as the day progressed, there were so many in the lagoon that the destroyer *Dashiell,* maneuvering for a firing run, narrowly averted collisions with the unwieldy landing craft.

Matters ashore were no less confused. Shoup's radio communication with his battalions was spotty. Transmitters and receivers had been damaged or destroyed; the radio operators were dead or wounded. Runners were used to carry messages between units. Daring, fleet-footed Leathernecks volunteered for that hazardous duty. Few of them lived out the day.

One runner was killed by a sniper only a few feet from the CP. A Marine machine gunner tried to pick off the sniper who was perched in a coconut tree. The Leatherneck fired burst after burst without scoring a hit on the hidden rifleman. In exasperation, the Marine shot the slender tree trunk in half. The leafy top part crashed, and the fall killed the sniper.

"Maybe I'm not much of a sharpshooter," the gunner told his assistant, "but I'll do as a lumberjack."

Anxieties ran high on the *Maryland,* where General Julian Smith awaited word about the invasion's progress. Although few reports came from the beaches, Lieutenant Colonel MacPherson and other Kingfisher pilots kept the general informed of the crisis ashore.

The general realized that more troops were needed on Betio. Even with the reinforcements already in boats, he did not have men enough to overwhelm the Japanese. At least one more regiment would be needed. "Uncle" Julian radioed his superior, "Howlin' Mad" Smith, on the *Pennsylvania* off Makin, and asked him to release the 6th Marines, which was being held as V 'Phib reserve. If "Howlin' Mad" denied the request, Julian Smith planned to form a scratch unit of cooks, bandsmen, and other specialists and lead them into battle himself. This drastic step proved unnecessary. A message soon came from the *Pennsylvania* stating that a transport carrying the 6th Marines was leaving for Tarawa at once.

Julian Smith then ordered 1st (Red) Battalion, 8th Marines (Major Lawrence Hays, Jr.), which had been in boats since daybreak, to prepare for a landing after dark. (The battalion was the last of the divisional reserve.)

At 1445 (2:45 P.M.) Smith queried Shoup by radio whether a night landing was feasible and where it could most effectively be made.

That message was never received at Shoup's CP and Red Battalion never got its orders to land. Adverse atmospheric conditions had briefly blocked radio reception. The radio operator aboard the *Pennsylvania* who sent both messages failed to check whether Shoup and Hays had received them.

As a result, Red Battalion was to spend the whole night in landing boats waiting for orders. An officer in Charlie (C) Company confessed, "We were so seasick and disgusted that we'd have thanked the Nips for shooting us."

91

(General Julian Smith, unaware that Hays had not received the landing order, believed Red Battalion was on the way to reinforce Shoup.)

The bellicose colonel was having his troubles; snipers and machine gunners on the *Saida Maru* were playing havoc with the men on Beach Red 2. At least a dozen Leathernecks had been killed by fire from the ship. Two Marines had fallen close to the CP and Shoup was very angry.

He cursed the lack of artillery which kept him from "blasting that lousy tub out of the water." But no amount of ranting could alter the fact that the Japanese in the ship were shooting down his men. Just before radio transmission failed, Shoup called for an air strike on the freighter.

A flight of SBDs slashed down and plastered the ship with bombs. The Dauntlesses were followed by strafing Hellcats. But the air attack did not accomplish the job. When the planes disappeared, the machine guns on the *Saida Maru* started shooting again.

At about 1600 (4:00 P.M.) Colonel Shoup sent Colonel Carlson out to the *Maryland* with a load of wounded in one of the few amtracs still operating. The Raider hero was making the hazardous trip so "Uncle" Julian might have a first-hand account of the situation on Betio. Shoup also wanted Carlson to tell Smith just what was needed on the beach: more men, water, ammunition, medical supplies, plasma, and artillery. All could be sent in to the pier down a narrow passage that was fairly safe from enemy fire. (Everyone hoped the tide would rise at night and flood the fringing reef.)

Carlson did not arrive aboard the *Maryland* until late in the evening. He delivered his report to General Smith and, at the CG's behest, turned in for a few hours of well-deserved rest.

But there was little sleep for the men on Betio. As daylight began fading, the Marines dug in for the night. A few units had advanced 200 or 300 yards inland. Most, however, were still pinned down at the seawall, and some had been stopped only 30 feet from the water.

Death and devastation was on every side. Slain Marines sprawled where they had fallen; wrecked amtracs, several still smoldering, jutted bow down in the water or lay on their sides like great wounded beasts. The sand was littered with battle debris: discarded packs, pierced helmets, rifles, cartridge belts, bloody shirts, shell casings, pieces of equipment. The stench of death and decay fouled the air and mingled with the smell of cordite and gunpowder. Not even the night breeze could clear out the putrid odors.

Pale pink Japanese tracers streaked across the deepening dusk from gun positions inland, and the Japanese kept spraying Beach Red 2 from the *Saida Maru*. They were answered by orange-red American tracers that made fiery lines in the gloom. An officer in Shoup's CP watched the trail of the enemy's pastel-tinted tracers. "That's a pretty color," he said.

"Aw hell, Lieutenant!" a Leatherneck sentry growled. "I'd be ashamed if I was a Nip. *Pink* tracers! Geez!"

All at once action flared up several miles out to sea. The sky was lit by red flashes, and the thudding of many guns reverberated across the water. For a while shooting ceased ashore. Marines stared out to the open water. Rumors of a major naval engagement spread among the Americans. But the firing ended as abruptly as it had begun. There had been no sea fight. Three Japanese "Kate" torpedo bombers had tried to sneak in for a night attack on the ships in the lagoon, only to be driven off by AA guns.

With full darkness, the Imperial Marines tried to locate individual American foxholes and used many ruses to trick the Leathernecks into exposing their positions. One Japanese who spoke good English called, "Somebody come help me! Where are you? I'm hit! I need help!"

"No you don't, Tojo! Not anymore!" a Leatherneck cried and flung a hand grenade. There was a blast, a scream, and then silence.

"The Nips must've figured we were green. Nobody fell for Tojo's tricks. We'd seen them all on Guadalcanal. Our guys wouldn't leave their foxholes for anything," a noncom said. "And they'd never fire a rifle to give away a position. We used grenades after dark. The Nips could never tell where they came from. We knocked off quite a few would-be infiltrators."

Transports and cargo ships drew off at night to designated positions for protection against submarine and air attacks. However, the destroyers *Ringgold, Anderson, Frazier,* and *Dashiell* patrolled Betio until dawn to give the Marines fire support if necessary.

Communications men finally strung telephone wire to link the CP with the battalions. This enabled Colonel Shoup to get a picture of what was going on. He learned that his 3,500 Marines held a front about 600 yards long and 300 yards in depth at its farthest inland point.

Defending this line was Major Crowe's White Battalion, 8th Marines, at Beach Red 3; Red and Blue battalions, 2nd Marines, under Major Wood Kyle and Lieutenant Colonel Walter Jordan (who still led Amey's troops), had pushed in a short distance on Beach Red 2. At Beach Red 1, Major Mike Ryan's two companies had hacked out a strip 200 yards deep and 100 yards wide on Betio's western tip. The survivors of Blue Battalion, under Major John Schoettel, came ashore late in the day after Ryan's men mopped up the Japanese who had blocked the landing.

The Marines had gained these footholds on Betio with blood and agony, their task made even more difficult by the tide which still refused to turn, even after sunset.

Under cover of darkness, the Marines brought in the supplies Shoup had requested through Colonel Carlson. Reinforcements straggled to land from the reef, inching their way in the black night. Artillerymen stripped down 75-mm howitzers and carried the pieces on their backs from the reef to Beach Red 2, where the guns were reassembled. Medics came with blood plasma, morphine, and bandages. Both officers and enlisted men lugged in many cases of rifle and machine-gun ammunition, mortar shells, and artillery shells.

Colonel Shoup, wracked with the pain of his wounded leg, worried that the enemy might launch a counterattack. He knew a determined charge could drive his men into the sea. Shoup had witnessed desperate *banzai* assaults on Gua-

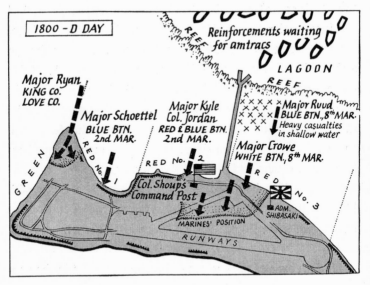

dalcanal and knew the fury of them. He warned his battalion commanders by telephone to remain doubly alert.

Marines in shallow foxholes needed no urging from officers to be watchful. Every man fully expected bands of wildly screaming Japanese to come rushing out of the darkness. They awaited the attack with readied rifles, grenades, bayonets, and knives. The Marines were tense with dread; sweaty hands clutched rifles; machine gunners sat with fingers curled around triggers peering into the black night until eyes ached.

But the enemy did not come.

"We wondered what Tojo had up his sleeve," a Marine said. "I'd fought the Nips on Tulagi and knew how they worked. If they didn't get you at the water's edge you can bet they'd counterattack at night. We didn't think much of our chances. If Tojo'd given us a good push, we'd have ended up in the middle of the lagoon."

The American line, consisting of isolated foxholes and small groups that had occupied abandoned pillboxes, was neither strong nor solid. All along the front, great gaps yawned. The flanks dangled in the air. "We were a perfect setup for a Nip knockout blow. We had nothing that could have stopped the enemy. It looked like a bad night for the Corps," a 2nd regiment officer remarked.

Rear Admiral Keiji Shibasaki had indeed planned his battle strategy as the Americans surmised he would. He meant to maul the invader on the beaches and then finish him off with a night attack.

But his troops had been staggered by the avalanche of U.S. naval shells; the bombardment and the air strikes had severed his lines of communications. All telephone lines were out and no radio was left undamaged. The forces were depleted. Although his brave men fought stoutly from strongpoints, they were scattered, and he had no way to mobilize them for a concerted blow.

Thus, Shibasaki had to be content with harassing the Yankees instead of crushing them. He stayed in his CP to prepare for the next day's action; from the safety of the bunker he heard his mortars lobbing shells onto the beach. His machine gunners peppered the Yankees, and bold snipers kept shooting at them from behind log barricades, palm trees, the *Saida Maru,* and wrecked amtracs.

The admiral was not dissatisfied with the results of the first day's fighting. Though he had lost many men—some units had met *zemmetsu*—his fighters had killed Yankees by the dozens and would kill more the next day. The Americans could expect no mercy from him. Blood for blood!

While the loss of communications hindered him, it was not he, but the Yankees, who tottered on the brink of destruction. Before another sun had set, Admiral Shibasaki promised his staff officers, not a single American would be left alive on Betio.

CHAPTER FOUR

THE DEATH STRUGGLE

SUNDAY, NOVEMBER 21, 1943–
TUESDAY, NOVEMBER 23, 1943

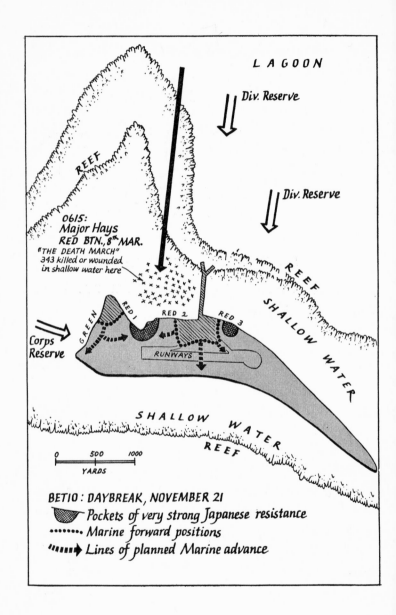

LAGOON

Div. Reserve

Div. Reserve

REEF

0615:
Major Hays
RED BTN., 8ᵀᴴ MAR.
"THE DEATH MARCH"
343 killed or wounded
in shallow water here

SHALLOW WATER

REEF

Corps
Reserve

GREEN

RED 1

RED 2

RED 3

RUNWAYS

SHALLOW WATER

REEF

0   500   1000
YARDS

BETIO: DAYBREAK, NOVEMBER 21

Pockets of very strong Japanese resistance

Marine forward positions

Lines of planned Marine advance

CHAPTER
FOUR

≣ |||||| 1

Shortly before daybreak of Sunday, November 21, the distinctive throbbing of a Japanese "Emily" flying boat sounded over Betio. A Marine in a foxhole cocked his head and listened.

"Well, I'll be damned! That's old 'Washing Machine Charlie' from Guadalcanal!" he exclaimed.

(During the Guadalcanal campaign, the Japanese made nightly nuisance attacks on the Americans with flying boats. The Marines had nicknamed the unwelcome visitors "Washing Machine Charlie" and "Louie the Louse.")

Men sat up and swore at the new "Washing Machine Charlie" flying back and forth. The pilot seemed unable to decide where the American lines were. After dropping three small bombs which splashed harmlessly in the water, he flew inland over the Japanese position and dumped a few bombs there. The Marines laughed as the plane chugged away in the night.

"Old Charlie wasn't taking any chances, was he? A bomb here and a bomb there. I guess he figured we had to be in one place or the other," a Leatherneck chuckled.

At the same time that "Washing Machine Charlie" was visiting the Marines ashore, someone in General Julian Smith's CP on the *Maryland* suddenly realized that nothing had been heard from Red Battalion, 8th Marines, for many hours. After some frantic radio queries (wireless communications had been restored), he found that Major Hays and his men had been on the landing boats all night long.

Colonel Shoup, also, had been wondering what had happened to Hays' battalion. He was in dire need of the troops. When he was told the men were still in Higgins Boats, Shoup "blew his top" according to an eyewitness.

However, he calmed down enough to request Hays to land on Beach Red 2, east of the pier, where Red and White battalions, 2nd Marines, were readying an attack to seize the airfield and push on to the south shore which would slice Betio in half.

At 0615 (6:15 A.M.) the first wave of Higgins Boats carrying Red Battalion, 8th Marines, grated onto the fringing reef. (The perverse tide still had not risen.) By then, only 18 amtracs were left, and these were busy evacuating wounded men from the beaches. They could not shuttle the reinforcements to shore from the reef. When the landing boat ramps clanged on the coral, men who had been at sea for more than 20 hours stumbled out to be met by deadly fire. Machine guns cut loose from the *Saida Maru,* dozens of automatic weapons opened fire from every direction, and mortar shells thudded like bass drums.

In moments the reef was slippery with the blood of dead, dying, and wounded Marines. "It was a massacre. The Nips slaughtered our guys," a survivor asserted bitterly.

Not every Marine was hit. Those who escaped the murderous volleys leaped into the water and waded to Beach Red 2, more than 500 yards away. Casualties were enormous; of the 199 men in the first wave, only 90 reached land. But the wade-in continued; not a man faltered. The trek through the water was called "The Death March" by those who took part in it. This was a repetition of the disaster that had befallen Blue Battalion, 8th Marines, the previous day.

The Marines in the Beach Red 2 sector watched the butchering of their comrades with horror, but they also fought ferociously to help them. Major Kyle led Red and Blue battalions, 2nd Marines in a furious attack to wipe out the pillboxes and bunkers shooting at the men in the water. (Red and Blue battalions had been consolidated into one unit under Major Kyle. Since Jordan had come ashore only as an observer from the 4th Division, Major Kyle took over command when the battalions merged.)

103

The 75-mm pack howitzers, now lined up hub-to-hub at the seawall, pounded away; but their shells merely glanced off the thick concrete walls of the blockhouses. The machine guns were slowly being knocked out by demolition and flamethrower teams. However, this was not being accomplished quickly enough. Kyle's men could advance only a few feet at a time; there were too many guns guarding the airfield. When the major radioed Shoup for more men, the reply was: "Do all you can with what you have. I can't help you."

Meanwhile the second and third waves of Higgins Boats with elements of Red Battalion, 8th Marines, had reached the reef, and the enemy guns were again making a death trap of the coral barrier. A Navy lieutenant told the men in one boat not to disembark at that time. "It's suicide," he said. "You'll never make it."

"No, sir. We're going in. They need us on the beach. Besides, this is what we get paid for. Come on, you guys!" a sergeant said.

Without another word, the Leathernecks raced out behind the sergeant, stumbling over the bodies of the first-wave men, and jumped into the water. The so-called Death March went on for nearly five hours until all of Red Battalion got ashore. At 1100 (11:00 A.M.) Major Hays reassembled his companies and marched out to join Kyle at the airfield. He had lost 343 men, 108 killed and 235 wounded —over 30 percent of the battalion's strength, but 600

104

Leathernecks still followed him; they vowed to make the enemy pay for their fallen buddies. "There wasn't one guy who hadn't lost a friend. The war became a very personal affair for every man in Red Battalion," an Able (A) Company officer said.

Throughout this landing operation, the guns on the *Saida Maru* had caused the most casualties. The hulk was bombed by SBDs, Hellcats strafed it, 81-mm mortars on shore lobbed shells onto the wreck, and a brace of 75-mm howitzers kept pummeling it, but nothing stopped the machine guns.

At last, a group of Marine demolition men volunteered to clean out the ship with TNT satchel charges. Joined by a detail of tommy-gun-wielding Leathernecks, they climbed into a rubber boat and paddled out to the freighter. The Japanese concentrated their fire on the small boat and there seemed no chance for the Marines to reach the *Saida Maru*.

Miraculously, they arrived unscathed and clawed up the vessel's canted side. The Leathernecks ran from porthole to porthole dropping in their lethal charges. The *Saida Maru* bucked and heaved at every detonation and the tommy gunners sprayed the insides of the ship with bullets. After a while, a tall Marine stood up on a spar that jutted from the tilted deck and waved his arms triumphantly. A ragged cheer rose from shore.

The *Saida Maru* was dead.

≡‖‖‖‖‖ 2

At the same time that Red Battalion, 8th Marines, was starting its frightful wade-in, Lieutenant William Hawkins of the S&S platoon appeared at the CP. He was ashen and in pain from his wounds; his fatigue jacket was stiff and caked with dried blood. But "The Hawk's" eyes still blazed defiantly and he steadfastly refused to let a corpsman attend him.

"Those jokers'll send me back," he told Colonel Shoup. "I came for orders, sir."

The tough CO, his thigh wrapped in a dirty, bloody bandage, grinned at Hawkins. "You're my kind of Marine, Lieutenant," Shoup said. He jabbed a grimy finger at a spot on the map. "The Nips have five machine guns in pillboxes here holding up the attack on the airfield. Can you get them for me?"

"Yes, sir. We'll give it a try."

"Okay, son. Good luck," Shoup said.

"The Hawk" saluted and left the CP. Despite all the fighting the S&S platoon had seen on D-Day, the unit was almost intact; its losses had been slight—one dead, three wounded.

The men were unwashed, hungry, thirsty, and tired but still ready for action. With "The Hawk" leading, they knocked out the Japanese guns by creeping up and flipping grenades into the pillboxes. But their triumph was not without a price. "The Hawk" received still another wound, a bullet in the chest. Someone else might have had enough and quit, but not the S&S platoon's CO.

Staggering to his feet he went after another enemy position and destroyed it. The platoon followed him and blasted two more guns.

But "The Hawk's" war was over.

A mortar shell landed nearby and riddled him with shrapnel. He was dying by the time stretcher bearers carried him away but still had strength enough to raise himself on one elbow and look back. The last thing he saw was a Marine patrol advancing across the airfield.

(When the strip was captured later that day, Colonel Shoup named it Hawkins Field for the man who had done so much to help take it and had given his life on an obscure island far from his Fort Scott, Kansas, birthplace.)

"Bill Hawkins died fighting for his country, which was the way he wanted to go," a fellow officer said.

Something favorable for the Americans was happening out at the fringing reef. The tide had started rising. If it went high enough, Higgins Boats and other landing craft could then ride over the reef and come straight to the beaches, bringing men and supplies. Marines would no longer have to wade in against enemy fire.

If only the tide rose high enough . . .

At 1100 (11:00 A.M.) it reached a depth to menace the wounded still lying on the coral. Swirling water lapped at them and threatened to drown the helpless Marines. Two launches from the transport *Sheridan* came to pick up the wounded. A Japanese sniper hidden in a wrecked Higgins Boat shot at the launches and the rescuers sped off, leaving 13 seriously wounded men still trapped by deepening water.

A shrapnel-and-bullet-scarred amtrac named *Old Lady* waddled to the reef. Her driver guided her gingerly about so his crewmen could haul in the wounded. All the while, the *Old Lady*'s gunner fought a bitter duel with the sniper. Disdainful of enemy bullets, the gunner triggered a burst that killed the sniper.

An officer who witnessed both gun fight and rescue reported: "the gunner, helmsmen, and crew of the *Old Lady* deserve the highest praise . . . for displaying courage under fire far beyond the call of duty. . . ."

Another example of a Marine's contempt for danger occurred at Shoup's CP where the exhausted colonel and his staff were running the battle. Shoup had plenty to worry about—Kyle's attack on the airfield; reports of ammunition, drinking-water, and ration shortages coming in from the field; the slow evacuation of casualties; the tide over the reef.

The tough Leatherneck was beginning to show the strain; an aide noticed that his hand shook when he held a telephone. Shoup seemed to have aged years in his hours on Betio; his face twisted with pain when he walked.

"We're in a tough spot. The Nips aren't cracking. The situation's lousy. And I don't know how much more our boys can take," he said.

Just then a dust-covered, grimy Private First Class (PFC) sauntered up to the CP. "He was the most unkempt young man I'd ever seen. The dirt on his face must have been a quarter of an inch thick," an officer in the CP remarked.

The Leatherneck strode right into the command post and grinned amiably at everyone. Strands of scraggly blond hair poking out from under his helmet made him look like a small boy.

"Hey! Anybody got some cigs? My machine-gun crew out yonder ain't had a smoke for hours. They're hungry for a butt," he said, unimpressed by either the officers or the bullets flicking past.

Someone tossed him an open pack of cigarettes. The PFC took one and lit it. He drew deeply and said, "That's more like it!"

"Son, what's your name?" Colonel Shoup asked.

"Adrian Strange."

"How old are you?"

"Twenty."

"Do you know who I am?" the CO said.

"Are you kidding? Of course I do. You're the Old Man. Don't fret, Colonel. We'll lick the Nips. We ain't even started to fight," PFC Strange said. "Why, take me. I just

109

got another sniper on the way here. That makes six this morning. And me practically a cripple. Stepped in a shell hole yesterday and twisted my ankle. Well, thanks for the smokes."

With a genial wave, Strange walked away from the CP. After he had gone a few yards, a bullet kicked up sand in front of him. He turned and grinned back at the gaping officers. "See that? Stupid sniper! He ain't anything to worry about. The bum couldn't hit a barn with a shotgun."

And, waving merrily, he was gone.

Colonel Shoup threw up his hands. "And I was concerned about the men. A kid like that—a kid like that— now there's a *Marine!*" he said. "As long as we have boys like him, we're okay."

There were scores of young Americans like PFC Strange on Betio—brash, impudent, reckless youths who looked into the face of danger unafraid. (They seldom lasted long in battle—Strange died of wounds later that day.) However, their devil-may-care boldness inspired less daring men. Not every Marine on Betio had the courage of "The Hawk" and Bordelon or the brashness of Strange.

In one sector an officer called on his men to take out a Japanese machine gun. He started with almost 100 Leathernecks following him, but on reaching the objective found that only two had come with him all the way; the rest had taken cover behind some trees. Yet, a little later, those same Marines stormed a blockhouse at bayonet point.

Marines, after all, were only ordinary youths—neither heroes nor cowards; some were braver than others; some broke in combat. But, on the whole, Colonel Shoup's Leathernecks—most of them only about twenty years old—when confronted by the worst ordeal young Americans had yet been called upon to face, came through with honor. . . .

≡≡≡|||||| 3

While the tide was rising on the fringing reef, Major Mike Ryan's two companies fought along Beach Green (Betio's western flank). The men, who had already earned for themselves the nickname "Ryan's Fighting Fools," were supported by the guns of two destroyers which rode in so close that they "scraped their bottoms."

The tin cans blasted Japanese strongpoints as King and Love companies forged ahead. When the destroyers' shells endangered the Leathernecks, the warships withdrew, and the attack proceeded, led by two Sherman tanks. One of them, *China Gal,* had already gained immortality for her work on D-Day.

The tanks ground cautiously onward, followed by files of Marines. However, the tank commanders had trouble spotting camouflaged pillboxes. *China Gal* came to a stop. The hatch clattered open and Lieutenant Ed Bales poked his head out.

"I need an intelligent man to spot targets for us," he called out to the Marines.

A sergeant shifted the cud of tobacco he was chewing, ejected a stream of tobacco juice, and drawled, "Heck, Lieutenant. I'm no ball of fire in the brains department, but I'm smart enough to know a pillbox when I see one. I'll do it!"

Equipped with a walkie-talkie, the sergeant went ahead of the tanks and pointed out one pillbox after the other. Armor-piercing shells from *China Gal* and her partner tore through the strongpoints. Leathernecks then finished the job with grenades, TNT, bayonets, and bullets. Gradually, the western beach was overrun and Ryan happily reported his success to the CP.

Meanwhile, Red and Blue battalions, 2nd Marines, had pushed beyond the airfield to Betio's southern coast. They held only a small salient and had to beat off furious counterattacks, but, for the first time since the initial landings, the Americans could be optimistic. No longer was the issue in doubt. It was now only a question of how long the enemy would continue to resist.

General Julian Smith, on the *Maryland,* called in Colonel Maurice Holmes, CO, 6th Marines, when that unit arrived at Betio. Smith gave Holmes two orders: one was to make a landing on Beach Green, now securely held by Ryan's intrepid fighters; the other was to land on the tiny islet of Bairiki, a short distance east of Betio, where some Japanese had been observed crossing over the coral strand. Smith wanted that escape route cut and a battery of 75-mm pack howitzers placed on Bairiki to shell the Japanese defending Betio's eastern tip.

White Battalion, 6th Marines, was given the Bairiki mission and units of it took off in Higgins Boats under the command of Lieutenant Colonel Raymond Murray. As they were approaching the objective, Hellcats swarmed over the little outpost where 15 Imperial Marines were manning a single pillbox mounting two machine guns.

For some reason, the Japanese had taken a drum of gasoline into the strongpoint with them; a stream of .50-caliber incendiary bullets from a Hellcat passed through an aperture and pierced the drum, which ignited and exploded. By the time Murray's men came ashore, they found only the smoldering debris of the pillbox and fifteen charred corpses. The pack howitzers were soon landed and put into action.

Red Battalion, 6th Marines, under Major William K. Jones, reached Beach Green in rubber boats. They poured ashore and were tearfully embraced by Ryan's battle-stained men. The newcomers wasted no time in emotional display, but moved through Ryan's haggard Leathernecks and dug in at the western end of the airfield. The vise was closing around Admiral Shibasaki, still in the CP bunker with his 300 men. In addition, many individual Japanese strongpoints still held out, and fighting never slackened.

However, Colonel Shoup earlier had sensed impending victory. He confidently radioed the *Maryland:* "Casualties many; percentage dead unknown; we are winning!"

The CO had good cause for showing such confidence. Although well aware that much hard combat was ahead, his jubilation was based on the turning of the tide at the reef. At last the waters closed with a rush to engulf the barrier.

A flotilla of landing craft raced to shore carrying troops and needed supplies. The only hindrance to their movement was sporadic rifle and machine-gun fire from Japanese positions in an area called "The Pocket."

This was the stretch of 600 yards from the CP to Beach Green yet held by the enemy. The Americans paid no more heed to the bullets than they would have to a swarm of gnats. These Japanese diehards proved more of an annoyance than a problem, although men were still being killed and wounded on the northern beaches.

The landing craft dumped their supplies on the sand and left loaded with casualties; for the first time since the invasion had begun, the wounded were no longer forced to wait agonizing hours for transportation to the ships and proper medical care.

Now that the reef could be crossed with ease, Admiral Hill appointed Captain John B. McGovern as boat-control officer to regulate traffic. Establishing a CP on board the minesweeper *Pursuit,* McGovern brought order out of chaos. Using a bullhorn, the captain issued commands to landing craft and directed supplies and reinforcements to points where they were needed.

Shermans and light tanks came on LVT's. They rumbled inland through great gaps blown in the seawall by engineers. Bulldozers rattled out of landing craft. The flames on the pier were extinguished and a procession of men and jeeps, towing fieldpieces, rolled unimpeded down its entire length.

Beachheads were widened and expanded in every sector, but the battle was far from over. This was brought sharply home to the men in the CP when an Imperial Marine, trapped in the pillbox that dominated Shoup's headquarters, crawled to a loophole and began shooting into the command post. He wounded a Marine corporal in the leg and everyone scrambled for cover.

"Get that Nip!" Shoup yelled, waving a pistol.

A dozen Leathernecks rushed to the pillbox and deluged it with hand grenades. No further shots came from that source, but those in the CP moved about warily, keeping an eye cocked at the shrapnel-marked stronghold.

Further inland, the Marines found solid proof that the foe had started to crack. By sunset, Japanese who only a few hours earlier would have fought to the last man and last bullet, were committing *jisatsu*—killing themselves. The Imperial Marines peered out of firing ports and saw the

115

advancing Leathernecks. They felt a sense of shame and failure; they had not destroyed the Yankees at the water's edge nor had they defeated them in battle. The Americans were winning and the dishonor was great.

Soldiers in a Western army might have surrendered, once it became obvious that resistance was futile. But these Imperial Marines, the elite of Japan's fighting men, these modern *Samurai,* had sworn a blood oath to win victory for the Emperor. Surrender was unthinkable; surrender was disgraceful, a loss of face.

So Shibasaki's men died at their own hands. *Jisatsu* was preferable to defeat. They used bayonets, grenades, rifles, and pistols to kill themselves. Perhaps, through mass *jisatsu,* the Imperial Marines hoped their spirits would be worshiped among Japan's warrior dead at the great Yasakuni Shrine.

The Americans approached the strongpoints, braced for the angry yammering of machine guns. Instead there was only silence. They rushed from one pillbox to another, staring at the dead enemy.

"I don't get it," a Leatherneck said. "Why should anyone do this? They could've kept on fighting and then surrendered when it became hopeless. Nothing's gained by committing suicide."

"Sure, but the Nips look at things differently, Mac. If you're defeated, you bring shame on your ancestors, your family, and yourself. Besides, you've let down the Emperor, so the only way out is to kill yourself. That's screwball thinking from our viewpoint, but it's the way the Nips see it," a second Marine explained.

"All right you guys, this is no place for a philosophical discussion. Let's go! There's still lots of Nips left with fight in 'em! Move out!" a sergeant bawled.

The Leathernecks slung their rifles and walked on. Up ahead enemy machine guns were chattering nastily. . . .

 4

The fighting continued throughout Sunday on the southern shore, where Major Kyle vigorously defended his perimeter. To the east, Crowe's men had pushed off the beach at last and were pressing inland toward Admiral Shibasaki's hulking, bombproof bunker-CP. "Ryan's Fighting Fools," backed by Red Battalion, 6th Marines, made swift progress in some sectors but were held up in others where the enemy resisted tenaciously.

At about 1800 (6:00 P.M.) a welcome visitor arrived at Colonel Shoup's CP. General Julian Smith had sent his Chief of Staff, Colonel "Red Mike" Edson, to take command of all troops on Betio.

Shoup greeted Edson warmly. For almost forty hours, without respite, he had been running the invasion; now he was relieved of that burden and could give full attention to his own regiment, the 2nd Marines, while "Red Mike" ran the main show.

Shoup's outfit had been badly mauled, as had all the regiments that landed on Betio. Dozens of the husky young Marines who had left Wellington only a few weeks before were dead or maimed. There had been a particularly high casualty rate among officers. Privates took over squads, corporals were commanding platoons, and sergeants were leading companies. The officer shortage created leadership problems, but the gaps were filled from the ranks.

Ordinary Marines, some only boys barely out of their teens, took over in the heat of battle, and the merciless struggle roared on. No man asked quarter nor expected any. It was a fight to the death and the combatants knew it.

Over in the Beach Red 3 area where Crowe's White Battalion, 8th Marines, was pushing south, an advance patrol sighted Shibasaki's bunker just as the sun began to set. The Marines stared at the gigantic bulk looming before them.

"Holy Cow! Do we have to take that?" a private whispered. "Why?"

The patrol's sergeant scratched his stubbly beard. "Because the Old Man says so. Maybe he'll change his mind when he sees it up close." He sent a runner back for Major Crowe. When the officer arrived, he studied the objective in the waning light.

"I want the navy to plaster that monster. We have to take

it in the morning and I'd like things to go as easily as possible," Crowe said.

He radioed for naval gunfire on the target. In response to his request a destroyer ran up the lagoon and came in perilously close to shore. Her 5-inchers pounded away. Concrete chips flew from the bunker as the shells struck. The tin can poured salvo after salvo until more than 80 shells had hit the bunker. Flames danced and twinkled on its coconut-log roof, but, when the destroyer had stopped shooting and the smoke had cleared away, Crowe looked through his night glasses and then lowered them, his face clouded with disappointment.

"They hit it, all right. But we could've done as well throwing rocks. I don't think all that shellfire even rattled the crockery. We can expect a tough job tomorrow," he said gruffly to mask his feelings.

"If it wasn't tough, they wouldn't have given it to us," the patrol sergeant growled. . . .

The shelling had caused little damage inside the bunker. Admiral Shibasaki sat at a field table sipping *sake* as the 5-inchers smashed against the stout walls, which were so thick that the explosions seemed muffled and far away. He mentally complimented his predecessor, Admiral Saichiro. The man had done a most superior piece of work; this bunker was a masterpiece; all the fortifications on Betio had been brilliantly conceived and completed. But genius was not enough; the Yankees had come and they had survived Shibasaki's best blows.

The *sake* must have tasted bitter to the admiral, for he knew Betio would soon fall, and with it all Tarawa. He had failed the Emperor, a disgrace for which he could atone only in blood. But Shibasaki did not hold with *jisatsu* or the more ritualistic form of suicide, *hara-kiri*.

There was a better death for a fighting man. He would lead his men in a *banzai* charge when the time was right. That was the true road to honor and glory; to die wielding a samurai sword and rushing at the foe. *Jisatsu* and *hara-kiri* were for those who had lost their will to fight.

Keiji Shibasaki was not such a man.

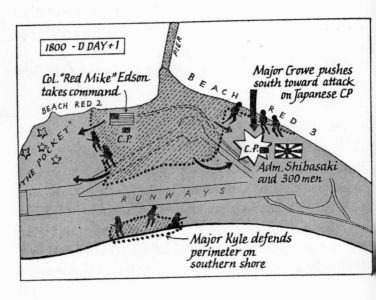

When morning came, he would show the Yankees that the price of victory had to be weighed in lives: so many young Americans must die for so many yards won. He drained the *sake* cup and signaled his orderly to refill it.

Actually, it was not he who had failed. The Yogaki plan was the cause of his downfall; that elaborate blueprint had crumbled to bits at the first touch like the brittle, yellowed pages of an ancient book.

No planes, no men, no submarines, no ships. Who had been left to stem the Yankee power? Keiji Shibasaki and his faithful, valiant men. Had it not been so unseemly, he would have wept for the gallant youths who had fallen in this cruel battle.

He still had the 300 fighters in the bunker. Next morning, they would follow him on the path that had no turning. For generations to come, every Japanese schoolchild would be taught the story of Shibasaki and his men. Songs would be sung about them, poems written, and prayers offered to the Imperial Marines who had given their lives for the Mikado on the distant Pacific isle of Betio in Tarawa Atoll.

He rose from his chair and walked slowly through the bunker as the shells burst on its roof and sides. His staff officers bunched behind him and followed the admiral.

Shibasaki toured all the firing posts. He spoke a word of encouragement to every rifleman and machine gunner. As he passed, men stood up and cheered him. *"Banzai! Banzai!"* they shouted, to show him they were undaunted.

121

The admiral ordered *sake* and sweet rice cakes for every man. He then carried out an unpleasant military obligation. It was his duty to inform the Imperial High Command in Tokyo of the garrison's fate. A radio transmitter had been repaired and the admiral sent the last message from Tarawa: "Our weapons have been destroyed. . . . From now on everyone is awaiting an opportune moment to attempt a final charge. Long live the Emperor! Long live Japan! *Banzai!*"

Having done this, Admiral Shibasaki retired to his quarters where he doffed his uniform cap and tied around his head a clean, white cloth known as a *hashamaki,* the Japanese warrior's traditional headdress. He checked his pistol and strapped a samurai sword around his waist.

There was nothing left but to wait and to think. . . .

≡≡≡ ||||||| 5

Monday, November 22. The day dawned hot. The sun hung in the sky like an angry red ball. Marines stirred out of their foxholes blinking in the pitiless sunlight. The heat was already so intense that thirst gnawed and many men unwisely drained their canteens.

The Leathernecks ate a tasteless breakfast of K rations and prepared for the day's fighting. Everyone from "Red Mike" Edson and Colonel Shoup to the lowliest rear rank private was amazed that the Japanese had not attacked dur-

122

ing the night. Except for a few infiltrators, the lines had been quiet.

That third day, the Marines seemed to realize the battle was at a new stage. The time of crisis for them had passed. It was no longer a question of hanging on to a few yards of blood-soaked beach; the danger of being pushed into the sea no longer existed. This day's combat would be one of coldly and precisely exterminating the enemy.

The tide rose even higher over the fringing reef. Boats passed above it; for all purposes, the barrier no longer even existed. Supplies were ferried ashore as though "trucked along a four-lane highway," which was how a former truck-driver from New Jersey described it.

The Burns Philp pier, where so many men had been killed, now shivered under rumbling traffic. Jeeps, tanks, weapons carriers, and bulldozers clanked and clattered on it from one end to the other.

The American offensive opened at 0700 (7:00 A.M.) when Red Battalion, 8th Marines, still smarting from the effect of the previous day's wade-in, jumped off in a westerly direction. Three light tanks led the assault. But, in the first minutes, a Japanese clutching a magnetic mine leaped out of a smashed pillbox and threw himself under the treads of the leading tank. The mine went off blowing up both the Japanese and the tank.

It soon became apparent that light tanks were not up to

the job of knocking out the many pillboxes that studded the route to the western flank of Betio. Their 37-mm guns did little more than chip the concrete. Half-tracks rushed in to support the tanks proved even less effective. After five hours, Hays' luckless battalion could report little success.

This was not the case on Beach Green where Red Battalion, 6th Marines (Major William K. Jones) rushed eagerly into battle. As eagerly, that is, as men could when faced with the distasteful mission of destroying strongpoints manned by a tough and skillful enemy. Major Jones had three Sherman tanks and a new tactical weapon—five bulldozers—which would introduce a novel method of attacking pillboxes.

The tanks waddled ahead, their 75's cracking open pillboxes as though they were giant walnuts. Behind the tanks came the Marines to finish off the enemy with grenade, flamethrower, bullet, or bayonet. When a pillbox proved too tough, Jones called on the bulldozers. After advancing with blades raised to ward off bullets, the 'dozer drivers shoveled piles of sand against the pillbox entrance, firing slits and air vents to bury the occupants alive.

Jones and his men swept eastward along the south shore until they linked up with Kyle at 1100 (11:00 A.M.). By then, Red Battalion, 6th Marines, had killed more than 250 Japanese and wiped out several dozen pillboxes at slight loss to themselves.

Before nightfall, Jones had advanced to the eastern end of the airfield. Except for that eastern tip, the bird's tail, all Betio's southern shore was now in American hands. A strongly entrenched force of Japanese still remained on the eastern portion of Betio. The coming of darkness prevented a final showdown. That had to be postponed until the next day.

Major Crowe's Leathernecks had advanced for their grand attack on Shibasaki's CP. The big bombproof was guarded on the right by a steel-encased pillbox which was apparently as impregnable as it looked. The bastion had "more machine guns than a porcupine has quills," according to one Marine. The Leathernecks eyed it uneasily. This was going to be a "tough one."

On the left of the CP stood a large coconut-log emplacement reinforced with concrete. That seemed to be an easier objective to attack. Before investing it, Crowe called for a barrage from his 81-mm mortars. The "stovepipes" were set up and zeroed in.

The very first shell that hit the coconut-log emplacement arched through a small opening, and the blockhouse disappeared in a series of violent, ground-trembling explosions.

The mortar gunners who had fired the round gaped in awe. "It was like the end of the world," a mortarman later said. "I knew the 81 packed a wallop—but nothing like that. It was as if all hell had busted loose. You never saw such fire and smoke. And the explosions rattled your teeth."

As the emplacement blew up, the force of the detonations crushed the steel pillbox, killing everyone in it. That mortar shell had landed squarely on a pile of ammunition, dynamite, and other high explosives stored in the emplacement.

The dust had barely settled when the doughty warhorse *Colorado* rolled up to the entrance of the main bunker. Her 75 belched, and the war-scarred tank shuddered under the recoil. Three shells, fired pointblank, slammed into the bunker's steel-reinforced door and Shibasaki's stronghold lay open to attack.

With a yell, the Leathernecks charged forward. The foe fought hard but could not stem that irresistible rush. A detachment of demolition men, armed with TNT satchel charges, led by young Lieutenant Alexander Bonnyman, swarmed up the sloping sides of the bunker to drop TNT down the air vents on the roof.

Imperial Marines tried to stop the Yankees. Bonnyman planted himself between them and his men. Firing his carbine from the hip, he barreled into the Japanese and the enemy fell back before him. He was bleeding from a dozen wounds, but his one-man foray had given the engineers time to place their charges.

The TNT ripped the insides of the bunker. Japanese came tumbling out and were shot down by American tommy gunners and riflemen. Then, the bulldozers moved in to seal off the bunker's exits. Flamethrowers squirted liquid fire through loopholes. From within the structure came horrendous screams, and then nothing. Admiral Shibasaki never made his *banzai* charge. He died inside the bunker with his men.

Stretcher bearers rushed Bonnyman to an aid station but the medics could not save him. "He died for us," Major Crowe said. "I'm putting him in for a Medal of Honor. It's not much against a man's life, but we have no other means to show our gratitude."

During the fighting at the Japanese CP, Blue Battalion, 6th Marines, commanded by Lieutenant Colonel Kenneth McLeod, landed on Beach Green and headed eastward across the islet on the heels of Crowe's men. The tempo of the American attack picked up speed; only in The Pocket were the Marines almost at a standstill.

During the early afternoon of November 22, Major General Julian Smith, accompanied by staff officers, left the *Maryland* in a launch and went ashore at Beach Green. After inspecting that sector, Smith and his party boarded one of the few working amtracs for the trip by water to "Red Mike" Edson's CP. On the way, they passed The Pocket where Hays was fighting. Enemy machine-gun fire struck the amtrac and the general had to fling himself prone while bullets hissed overhead.

By the time Smith left the alligator, he seemed convinced

the battle was far from over. Edson and Shoup tried to assure him that last-ditch enemy resistance would be quickly overcome, but their arguments lost much force when a lone sniper fired into the CP from the ruined pillbox.

A deadly game of hide-and-seek then followed. Marines chased the daring rifleman, who apparently was gifted with the ability to "hide behind a grain of sand," according to one of his pursuers.

Colonel Shoup stood at the entrance to the CP, pistol in hand, and barked orders at the men trying to get a bead on the elusive foe. At last he shouted impatiently, "Do you want me to go out there and shoot him?"

A Marine who had known Shoup for more than 20 years

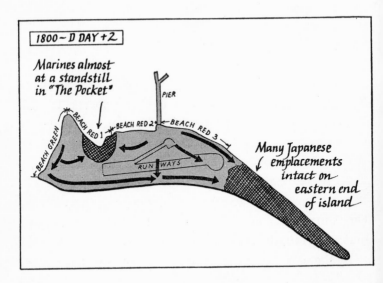

in the Corps told him, "No siree! We don't want you shooting at nobody, Colonel. It'd be too dangerous—we've seen you shoot. No siree! You just stay put. We'll get that Nip."

"Okay. See that you do," Shoup grinned. "The general's getting a bit jumpy."

"Tell 'Uncle' Julian to take it easy. We'll get the Nip," the old-timer said.

A few minutes later, the sniper was pursued and shot. But such bold enemy activity close to the CP, plus reports that more than 50 percent of the officers in the six assault battalions had been killed or wounded, caused General Smith to send a gloomy message to Brigadier General Leo Hermle, his assistant division commander. Smith said:

> *Situation for a rapid clean-up of Betio unfavorable. High casualties among officers make leadership problem difficult. Many emplacements intact on eastern end of the island. In addition, many Japanese strongpoints to westward of our front lines within our positions that have not been reduced. Progress slow and extremely costly. Complete occupation will take five days more. . . .*

 6

The Marines in the thick of battle did not share "Uncle" Julian's pessimistic outlook. On the contrary, even the men in The Pocket stopped at nightfall full of confidence; they scoffed at rumors of terrible losses. According to one story, the combined strength of Red and White Battalions, 8th Marines, was only 104 men; Blue Battalion of that regiment, the stories went, had been almost completely wiped out.

The Leathernecks on Betio were in no mood to hear such tales. They had gone through the day with relatively few casualties and had hurt the enemy severely. Nothing could dampen their soaring spirits—not the miseries of combat, the sickening foulness of decay in the air, nor their own weariness.

Veteran fighters, such as those in the 2nd Marine Division, had, through experience, developed a battle perception that alerted them to the imminence of victory. The Japanese suicides, the comparative ease with which pillboxes now fell, the growing piles of supplies on the beaches; all were harbingers that the end was near.

Yet as the men dug their foxholes that night, they knew the climax had not been reached. There still had to be the final confrontation, the last obligatory act. Men who had been on Guadalcanal bet among themselves that the enemy was going to make a *banzai* attack that night.

"The Nips'll come," a noncom prophesied. "I feel it in my bones."

"That's your rheumatism, Sarge," someone laughed.

There was light talk and banter, but the sentries were doubly alert and every man made sure his weapons were

130

handy before settling down. If the attack was to come it would be from the island's eastern end where the enemy had his only sizable force.

Red Battalion, 6th Marines (Major William K. Jones), held the right (southern) flank of a 400-yard line that crossed Betio at the narrow eastern end of the airfield. The left (northern) flank was manned by the thinned ranks of Major Crowe's White Battalion, 8th Marines.

The Japanese came after darkness fell. At 1930 (7:30 P.M.) a group of about 50 Japanese crept past an American outpost and crawled into positions occupied by Baker (B) Company, 6th Marines, commanded by Lieutenant Norman Thomas.

Marines and Japanese were locked in hand-to-hand combat for almost half an hour. Knives, rifle butts, and grenades were used until the Japanese fled. The artillery battery on Bairiki swept the terrain between the lines and killed the attackers to the man. Only a few Marines had been wounded, despite the fierce fighting.

The Americans quickly moved to reinforce the sector. Major Wood Kyle rushed a company to back up Jones, and Lieutenant Colonel McLeod hurried men into reserve positions. Everyone was tense; all thoughts of sleep had gone. Every movement in the darkness was taken for enemy infiltrators closing in for the kill.

But when the Japanese returned, it was not by stealth. At

131

2300 (11:00 P.M.) they burst out of the hummocks and rocks that covered the eastern part of the island, shouting, *"Banzai!"* It was a furious assault, led by sword-brandishing officers. The Imperial Marines threw grenades and fired at random. The Americans rose to meet the attackers. Automatic rifles, tommy guns, and machine guns mowed down the fanatical Japanese. The charge wavered and broke under the murderous fire; the foe fled to his own lines. Again, the Bairiki artillery cut loose. The 75's killed and wounded many Japanese. In the stillness that followed the clamor of battle, the Leathernecks could hear wounded men moaning and screaming between the lines. But this was no moment for pity. Word was passed from foxhole to foxhole to be ready for still another onslaught.

"The Nips haven't thrown the big one yet. Keep on your toes," Major Jones warned his men.

The "big one" came at 0400 (4:00 A.M.), Tuesday, November 23. Red rockets trailed up from the Japanese lines and then wild, keening yells, such as few Marines on Betio ever had heard before, shattered the night. Out of the darkness voices shrilled, "Yank you die! *Banzai!*" Whistles blew. The attack was on. At least 300 Japanese rushed from holes and pillboxes and hurled themselves on the Americans.

Baker (B) Company took the full force of the charge. A platoon sergeant later recalled: "It seemed as though all the Nips in the world had dropped down on us. We couldn't shoot fast enough to knock 'em off!"

132

The screeching foe overran Baker Company's outposts and broke into the main defensive perimeter. There, the worst fighting on Betio took place. Americans and Japanese grappled in a cursing, swirling affray. Men gouged, kicked, punched, and battled each other with every weapon from bayonets to rocks. One husky Marine automatic rifleman held his gun by the barrel and swung it in a blurring arc. He brained half a dozen Japanese with the heavy butt before he was bayoneted to death.

The struggle had no form or shape; there was neither front nor rear to the battle. At the height of it, Baker Company's CO frantically called battalion H.Q. for help. "We're killing them as they come at us, but we can't hold much longer. We need reinforcements!"

Major Jones replied: "You've got to hold, Norman! I can't spare a man! You've *got* to hold!"

Somehow, Baker Company held. When the Japanese fell back to regroup, they were pounded by artillery which dropped within 50 yards of the American lines. Farther off, the destroyers *Schroeder* and *Sigsbee* blasted the enemy's assembly area with 5-inch shells.

By 0500 (5:00 A.M.) the *banzai* charge had been smashed. The men of Baker Company looked about in wonderment; they had held and beaten off the suicidal foe.

"Man, that was something," a bone-tired Marine said.

As the sky lightened, troops from Blue Battalion, 6th

133

Marines, moved in to relieve Red Battalion. McLeod's men, who had not yet been in combat, stared at the carnage.

"Golly, Mac, it must have been rough," a Love Company man said to a Marine from Baker Company.

"Don't you believe it. We had a tea party," the battle-stained Leatherneck grunted.

A tally showed that more than 200 Japanese had been killed within the Marine lines; the artillery and ships' guns accounted for another 125.

On all Betio, only 500 Japanese still lived and their time was growing short. . . .

≡‖‖‖‖‖   7

When the American attack started at 0700 (7:00 A.M.), Tuesday, November 23, with carrier planes zooming down to pound the enemy positions in The Pocket, every Marine knew the ordeal was almost over. The *banzai* charge of the previous night had broken the enemy's back.

The planes swept back and forth for about half an hour; then the guns on Bairiki and Betio opened up. The fleet bombarded the eastern redoubt—16-inchers boomed and 5-inchers snarled as the bird's tail was bombarded from both ocean and lagoon. The naval guns thundered for fifteen minutes. The barrage lifted and the Leathernecks jumped off.

Lieutenant Colonel McLeod's Blue Battalion, 6th Marines, was in the van. The freshest troops on the island, these men went into battle jauntily, in sharp contrast to the slumped and weary Marines of the other battalions.

McLeod's men advanced behind *Colorado* and *China Gal,* with seven light tanks guarding the flanks. The two Shermans banged away at any target that could be found. The advance speeded up as the Marines met little resistance. The enemy fired sporadically at the Yankees, and then committed *jisatsu.* In the first five minutes of his attack, McLeod gained 150 yards.

One wing was held up briefly by a complex of bombproofs; satchel charges and flamethrowers soon eliminated these. Finally, only one stronghold remained. Lieutenant Lou Largey brought his tank *Colorado* up into position. The dependable Sherman shelled the bastion until the doors caved in. A band of 100 Japanese ran out, only to be shot down by many rifles and tommy guns. McLeod's Marines then marched, unhindered, to the very end of the bird's tail and splashed across the coral to Bairiki.

Major Hays fought through The Pocket to link up with "Ryan's Fighting Fools." The combined force destroyed the enemy to the last man. This was the final organized action on Betio. During that action the Americans killed 475 Japanese while losing only 9 dead and 25 wounded. At 1312 (1:12 P.M.) "Red Mike" Edson officially declared Betio was secured.

The battle was over. . . .

Blue Battalion, 6th Marines (Lieutenant Colonel Raymond Murray), cleaned up the rest of Tarawa Atoll by marching from Bairiki in the south to Lone Tree Island at the opposite end of the atoll. By November 28, the American flag fluttered from a tall coconut palm at Tarawa's northernmost point. During this operation, the Marines killed 175 Japanese. American casualties numbered 32 dead and 59 wounded.

(Operation Boxcloth, the code name for the capture of Abemama, had proceeded without a hitch. Sixty-eight Marines under Captain James Jones, the brother of Major William Jones, landed there from the submarine *Nautilus* right on schedule, the night of November 20. Natives on Abemama told them that only 23 Imperial Marines manned the island's defenses. These Japanese killed themselves after a brief skirmish with Jones and his men. On November 26, the Stars and Stripes was raised over Abemama. Farther north, Makin also fell to the Americans after a brief, but bitter, battle in which the 165th Infantry killed 445 Japanese at a cost of 66 dead and 152 wounded.)

The Battle for Tarawa had been a great American victory; the 2nd Division Marines killed 4,690 Japanese and successfully stormed an atoll which the enemy considered impregnable. It had not been an easy triumph; mistakes had been made and lessons learned at considerable price: 980 U.S. Marines and 29 sailors lost their lives at Betio and of the 2,311 American wounded, many were maimed for life and many would die of their injuries.

Except for minor mopping up of last-ditch diehards and the melancholy task of burying the dead, the battle was done; the Marines had completed their mission, and another battle streamer was added to the 2nd Division's colors.

On Wednesday, November 24, most of the men who had stormed Betio were preparing to leave it. They shuffled toward the beaches in ragged ranks. Boats were waiting to take them to the transports. Perhaps these youthful warriors wept silently for friends who had fallen; perhaps the awful panorama of the past three days still crowded their thoughts. They had added glory to the Corps; never had Marines fought such a battle.

There was glory indeed. "The Hawk," Bill Bordelon, and Alex Bonnyman would be awarded posthumous Medals of Honor; Colonel Shoup would live to wear his.

But glory seemed empty as the long columns stumbled across the shattered island. The dead lay unburied, Japanese and American locked forever in mortal combat. Ruin and destruction were everywhere. Smoke still rose from uncounted fires and the earth was torn, the trees shattered. But even as the Marines marched away, bulldozers were busy filling in shell holes on the airfield and a Seabee construction battalion had begun preparing the base for occupying troops that would soon be coming.

The Marines were fighting men. They could not dwell on war's horrors or its ironies. And there was irony. When they arrived at the beach, a surprise awaited them.

The tide had swept in and high water covered the sand to the top of the seawall. The transports were anchored close to shore and the fringing reef was buried under many feet of water.

Nature had played its bitter joke.

Had there been such a high tide when the invasion started, all the suffering and dying on the reef would not have occurred.

"Aw, what's the difference?" a Marine said, staring at the deep water. "High water on the reef would've meant high water at the seawall and no place for us to find cover. You never get the breaks in war."

So the Marines clambered into the boats and were ferried out to ships that would carry them from Tarawa, and on to battles yet unfought. . . .

BRIEF GLOSSARY OF MILITARY
ABBREVIATIONS

AA—	Antiaircraft cannon
AB—	Anti-boat gun
AKA—	Attack cargo ship
AP—	Armor-piercing shell
APA—	Attack transport
BLT—	Battalion Landing Team
CINCPAC—	Commander-in-Chief Pacific Fleet
CNO—	Chief of Naval Operations
CO—	Commanding Officer
CP—	Command Post
CTF—	Commander Task Force
CTG—	Commander Task Group
HE—	High Explosive Shell
JCS—	Joint Chiefs of Staff
LCI—	Landing Craft, Infantry
LCT—	Landing Craft, Tank
LCVP—	Landing Craft, Vehicles and Personnel
LST—	Landing Ship, Tank
LVT—	Landing Vehicle, Tracked (amphtrac, amtrac, amtrack)
ONI—	Office of Naval Intelligence
RCT—	Regimental Combat Team
TF—	Task Force
UDT—	Underwater Demolition Team

CASUALTIES IN BATTLE OF TARAWA

United States

U.S. Marines	Officers	Enlisted Men
Strength of Marines, Tarawa	811	15,987
Killed in Action	49	822
Wounded in Action	110	2,186
Died of Wounds	8	82
Missing, Presumed Dead	0	27
Wounded, Presumed Dead	0	2
Combat Fatigue	1	14
	168	3,133

Japanese

Strength of Japanese, Tarawa	4,836
Prisoners captured (Japanese)	17
Prisoners captured (Laborers)	129
Escaped	0
Japanese killed, Tarawa	4,690
	4,836
Japanese garrison, Abemama	23
Japanese killed, Abemama	23

(SOURCE: Capt. James R. Stockman, *The Battle of Tarawa:* Marine Corps, Historical Monographs, Washington: Government Printing Office, 1947)

TYPES OF AIRCRAFT USED AT TARAWA

United States

B-24 (Liberator)	Army, 4 engines, heavy bomber
	(Known as PBY-4 in Navy)
F6F (Hellcat)	Navy, 1 engine, fighter
OS2U (Kingfisher)	Navy, 1 engine, scout-observation
SB2C (Helldiver)	Navy, 1 engine, divebomber
SBD (Dauntless)	Navy, 1 engine, divebomber
TBF (Avenger)	Navy, 1 engine, torpedo bomber

Japanese

Mitsubishi Zero-1 (Betty)
Navy, 2 engines, high-level or torpedo bomber
Kawanishi Zero-2 (Emily)
Navy, 4 engines, patrol bomber (flying boat)

SUGGESTIONS FOR FURTHER READING

In gathering the material for this book, I consulted unit histories, personal letters, diaries and journals, ships' logs, and combat reports not easily available to the general reader. However, anyone who desires to read further about this battle will profit from the following books:

Blankfort, Michael. *The Big Yankee: A Biography of Evans Carlson*. Boston: Little, Brown, and Co., 1947.

Crowl, Philip A., and Love, Edmund G. *Seizure of the Gilberts and Marshalls*. Washington: Government Printing Office, 1955.

Hough, Lt. Col. Frank O. *The Island War: The U.S. Marines in the Pacific*. Philadelphia and New York: J. B. Lippincott Co., 1947.

Johnston, Richard W. *Follow Me! The Story of the Second Marine Division in World War II*. New York: Random House, 1948.

Morison, Samuel Eliot. *Aleutians, Gilberts and Marshalls* (*History of United States Naval Operations in World War II*, Vol. VII). Boston: Little, Brown and Co., 1960.

Pratt, Fletcher. *The Marines' War*. New York: Wm. Sloane Associates, Inc., 1948.

Sherrod, Robert. *Tarawa: The Story of a Battle*. New York: Duell, Sloan and Pearce, 1944.

Stockman, Captain James R. *The Battle for Tarawa*. (Marine Corps Historical Monograph.) Washington: Government Printing Office, 1947.

Newspapers for the week of November 21–28, 1943, and news periodicals for November and December, 1943, may be consulted for additional information about the battle for Tarawa.

INDEX

143

INDEX

ABOUT THE AUTHOR

Irving Werstein has made writing both his goal and his life. Even when he was officially a factory worker, a salesman, or an actor and comedian, Mr. Werstein spent his free moments writing.

He served in the U.S. Army from 1941 to 1945 and was a correspondent for *Yank* magazine. After the war he devoted all his time to writing; he has written magazine stories, radio and television scripts, and a number of books.

Mr. Werstein was born in Brooklyn, New York, and has lived in Mexico, Italy, and England. He has traveled extensively in Holland, Denmark, and France. He now lives in New York City.